The
Paranormal
Year
1993 Edition

The Paranormal Year

1993 Edition

JENNY RANDLES

ROBERT HALE · LONDON

ISBN 0 7090 4955 2

Robert Hale Limited
Clerkenwell House
Clerkenwell Green
London EC1R 0HT

Photoset in Ehrhardt by
Derek Doyle & Associates, Mold, Clwyd.
Printed in Great Britain by
St Edmundsbury Press Ltd, Bury St Edmunds, Suffolk.
Bound by WBC Bookbinders Ltd, Bridgend, Mid-Glamorgan.

Contents

Introduction

The paranormal fascinates people, from its all too visible enigmas such as UFOs and crop circles to the rather more cerebral puzzles offered by mind, space and time. In its own unique way each challenges our evolving view of how the universe functions.

Of course, there are things which people believe to be true which ultimately prove to be illusion; indeed some that turn out to be self-delusion. However, it can still be exciting to sift through the wreckage of all those shattered theories to figure out what really was going on.

For every mystery that falls by the wayside there is one which might help revolutionize science. Modern nuclear physics has its distant roots in alchemy. Psychology, to some degree, grew out of the reading of people's character practised by the first astrologers. In these cases what began as superstition, whilst not entirely crumbling, has been replaced by a new, hard science far removed from ancient myths.

Yet there remain new phenomena stalking the haunted borderland of human understanding where the bridge into rationality has not been crossed. If what today we call the paranormal does point toward real knowledge, then science has yet to embrace that fact. What we know about these mysteries depends upon those who continue to collect accounts of the eerie and the strange then dare to ask the shortest and most profound question in the English language – 'why?'

From the maelstrom of knowledge, theory and belief thousands of books have emerged, many of which contradict one another. Finding your way through the maze is far from easy. This volume aims to help. It sets out to review a single year's events from all around the world across a wide range of very strange phenomena. In a sense it presents a snapshot of the supernatural as it appeared during the calendar year of 1992.

I will describe key events in addition to the evidence, assess major research developments and experiments that were tried, the latest theories that researchers proposed, the results of the conferences held and the best of the published literature, from major books to the lively magazine circuit. As a result you will get a peek behind the scenes of what proved to be a fascinating year.

Of course, in a fast-moving subject all things change and nothing can ever be bang up to the minute. In addition, books take some time from writing to publication. But we can try to offer a digest of who said what, and who did what, throughout an amazing twelve-month spell.

In effect, this book is an annual report on the paranormal world as it stands in the wake of 1992. Seeing one year in sharp perspective in this way is rather like holding a mirror that reflects every other.

The Paranormal Year is divided into sections, ranging over ten major areas of research. These cover quite a spectrum: from alien animals to UFOs and from crop circles to earth mysteries. I had to draw the line somewhere, but tried to include any field of research that was not entirely subjective. I decided to exclude anything not amenable to hard scrutiny but which depended upon faith. This was not to deny validity to any belief but simply to retain an element of consistency in this report. If you have suggestions about topics that I missed, then please tell me about them so they can be considered for future editions.

Each of the sections will describe some of the best evidence, research and ideas that emerged during 1992, without being one-sided. Although this is a book about the evidence *for* the paranormal, important contributions from sceptics will be covered. I am not out to prove anything or to support one theory above another. As a long-standing writer in the field it would be foolish to suggest that I do not think some strange things are going on, but I also believe it is important to retain an open mind. To do that attention must be given to the more sensible ideas from the critics and detractors.

I will also look at how the year was reflected by the media; assessing how the predictions made about 1992 matched up with the year that entered our history books.

I have included a 'top ten' of the most important cases. My choice is subjective and unlikely to match your own. But if, as possible, some cases that look impressive eventually prove somewhat less than that after long investigation, then it will be my judgement that was at fault, not the evidence itself.

The supernatural *is* supernatural only because nobody has yet found what turns events we call strange into those we regard as normal. In time all things succumb. Even the oddest riddle has an answer somewhere.

This book is credited to my authorship, but I merely wrote it. That would have been impossible without the hundreds of people whose ideas and investigations come together and form the paranormal year of 1992. Rather than list every one of them, I have attempted to credit them wherever I can within the text. They do deserve it, so forgive any slight tedium this might suggest. References are given to such work and the details of various paranormal publications offered so that you can go back to source or seek new mysteries within their pages.

This specialist literature is not in the bookshops or newsagencies but is the life-blood of real paranormal research. It deserves wider attention by those who wish to probe these matters. If I missed your publication in this book and you would like to bring yourself to the notice of the world – or, indeed, if you have had a paranormal experience after 1992 and would like to pass that on for the consideration of others, then send details to me at:

37 Heathbank Road, Stockport, Cheshire, SK3 OUP.

I hope you find this book a useful reference to what proved to be a dramatic year and that it helps show how there are some pretty odd things going on around us all the time.

To see them all we need do is open up our eyes, and then our minds.

Jenny Randles
Cheshire
March 1993

Anomalies of Science

This section will cover an assortment of mysteries that came to the fore during 1992 and which do not neatly slot into any identifiable area of research. They represent anomalies of science which have not yet been completely resolved but may well eventually become incorporated into a discipline such as astronomy or meteorology. Time, and no doubt a lot of work, will tell.

American scientist William Corliss is the master of these fringe areas. He regularly culls the specialist press of various obscure technical magazines for what he calls his 'Sourcebook Project'. Ongoing reports are issued, updating mysteries from the realms of physics, meteorology, zoology and others (see details in the reference section).

The next few pages are much more modest than such a huge cataloguing programme, which I heartily recommend to you. Instead we will pick up on just one or two riddles that grabbed attention throughout the year.

I have made a decision not to say much about my own books in this text. To do so would be unreasonably immodest and if I singled out their findings it would be hard for you to judge whether I was being wholly objective or not (indeed, to be honest, it would be rather difficult for me to claim to be objective). So, generally speaking, I will leave it up to your discretion whether you seek them out or not.

However, it is necessary to mention one of them. As to how good or bad it was you must judge from very different reviews in sources such as the *New Scientist, Fortean Times*, the *Skeptic* magazine or a piece by Colin Wilson in the *London Standard* (mostly written in July 1992). None the less I refer to it as it was instrumental in bringing an area of the paranormal to life which had been sadly neglected for too long. The book, and its topic, was *Spontaneous Human Combustion* (Robert Hale) which I wrote with my friend and co-researcher Peter Hough.

The very idea of someone bursting into flames and being consumed to ash seems ridiculous. Indeed, according to a column in the *Skeptic* (January 1993), at a 1992 sales conference when our book was offered to paperback publishers, the literary world allegedly fell about in laughter. Although it seems this was at least partly because of a pre-arranged stunt where the sales rep started to emit smoke into the room! This subject was treated as a joke. Well, it is no joke to the victims of this grisly fate. Neither is it funny to their families who must face up to the consequences.

In a typical case, a person is found after a period of some hours so severely burnt that little more than a pile of cinders remains. Possibly one foot is intact, but the damage from this fierce blaze is extraordinarily localized. The carpet and furniture surrounding the deceased is often almost unaffected. In one instance plastic tiles directly underneath the utterly consumed body were not even warped.

It is easy to scoff at this phenomenon. Peter and I found much of that when we set out to talk in public about the subject in the summer of 1992. However, we also noticed a decided morbidness attaching itself to this matter rather more than it does to other aspects of the supernatural. It seems that people prefer not to think about it at all. Superficially this might be because it concerns death and we all prefer to avoid the tricky subject of mortality. On the other hand we speculate freely about ghosts or haunted houses, which involve the same kind of contemplation. So there is something unique about SHC (spontaneous human combustion) that scares the pants off people.

That said, we discovered in our research that, real or not, and we do not know which description applies, there is at least a case to be answered. We talked with fire officers, coroners, scene-of-crimes police investigators and others in the 'firing line' and there were many instances where the idea of SHC did not fit the facts. But there were also cases where it could not be ruled out and where other options failed to do justice to the suddenness or totality of the destruction.

Although from a perusal of fire death statistics it seemed possible that as many as a hundred cases potentially diagnosable as SHC may well occur every year, not one was recorded for 1992. This is a glaring anomaly. I doubt that this is because there were no suspect cases. So what happened? It is an example of the hidden nature of strange phenomena. Very often to find them you have to dig deep. They may not surface of their own accord.

Ball lightning

This is a favourite phenomenon of paranormal researchers, because it represents a subject that has crossed the boundaries from their field into what is now scientific respectability. From being a part of mystical claptrap a century ago it has entered the realms of physics and gets discussed in mainstream journals. As such it may point the way that other areas of speculation can follow to become legitimate sons of science.

In the earlier part of this century it was constantly argued that ball lightning was not a real phenomenon. Instead it was a misperception of ordinary lightning, perhaps creating a flash on the retina which seemed to persist for some time. There was no theory which predicted how a ball of energy a few inches in diameter could appear, either outside during a thunderstorm, or sometimes indoors on a calm day, and then drift about freely before exploding or vanishing after a few moments.

However, eventually the observations grew and some scientists joined the witnesses. Papers began to pass the rigid screenings of the serious literature and a few scientists proffered ideas. It took a couple of decades, and even now there are perhaps as many detractors as there are believers within the scientific community. But at least it is no longer quite the taboo subject that it was and a few brave souls, such as Dr Paul Davies, a physicist at Adelaide University, have pointed out two things.

Firstly, that the solution to the puzzle of ball lightning might add substantially to our knowledge of unusual energies and even pave the way towards technological breakthroughs. But, possibly more contentiously, that many ball lightning reports sound rather like examples of UFO sightings ... so what if some of those ridiculed UFO spotters have in reality made important observations of what might prove to be genuine scientific phenomena? Can physics afford to reject them all?

*

During 1992 the debate continued. A typical ball lightning case struck the area near Straide in Eire on the night of 20 March 1992. It came just after 10 p.m. during a fierce thunderstorm.

A family who live in the village of Knockmore reported to local meteorologist Martin Sweeney that a sphere about six inches in diameter appeared inside their house. It hovered about five feet above the ground and was visible for some ten seconds. The power was cut off because of a previous lightning strike but whilst the ball hovered it caused a local surge, presumably by way of induction. This made lightbulbs glow brightly, then explode as the power increased. The ball lightning itself vanished by elongating at the edges and disappearing in a silent flash of light.

TORRO (the tornado and storm research bureau) often features investigations of activity in their *Journal of Meteorology* (henceforth *J.Met*). Their ball lightning consultant is physicist Mark Stenhoff. He followed up a case that occurred just after 6 p.m. on the evening of 12 August 1992 at Conwy in North Wales.

One witness was a 30-year-old woman who was indoors during a period of heavy rain and hail but no lightning when a blue light entered through the window and actually struck her on the ankle. She was blasted across the room by the impact but was largely unscathed, even though she required hospital treatment for shock. A neighbour opposite was also struck at the same time and she suffered slight burns to the chest. The electrical wiring and telephone in her bungalow were damaged as a result of what seems to have been side flashes off the main ball which struck a tree and ripped the bark apart.

An eyewitness confirmed through her window that this was not an isolated ordinary lightning strike. She describes how a ball of 'white fire' akin to a meteor or comet flew horizontally along her driveway. It was football-sized and was like a fluorescent tube to look at but with tinges of yellow and a blue halo around the rim.

The object was in view for about fifteen seconds as it drifted silently towards the oak tree at only a few feet above ground level. It was close enough to observe that it was rotating slowly around its axis as it moved. When it hit the tree there was a massive explosion; the ball shrank and rolled down the trunk, splitting into feelers of electricity which earthed themselves in 'waves' of energy which then emitted sparks as a result.

During 1992 the big debate in the ball lightning world focused on a novelty – a photograph that was alleged to depict the phenomenon. These are extremely rare, since this is a very transient occurrence (just like a UFO, in fact). As a result movie or video film of a verified event is as yet non-existent.

The contentious case under the microscope (*J. Met*, March 1992) was investigated by Dr Alex Keul of Salzburg University. It actually occurred at Aussergant in the Montafon Valley in Vorarlberg, Austria as long ago as 1978 but, as is so often the case, took time to find its way into scientific hands.

The photographer, who runs a tourist house, submitted the single colour slide following a media appeal for evidence by Dr Keul, who then visited the site, famous for its Alpine ski resorts, to conduct an enquiry. He then sent copies of his report for independent assessment by four scientists each looking at the evidence from very different perspectives.

The camera, focused on infinity, was being used to take time exposures of a lightning storm over the adjacent mountains. Almost as soon as the shutter was pressed for one such exposure the cameraman heard a noise like a 'wire brush' being scraped and saw a ball of fire fall to the ground. He was so surprised that he released the shutter switch prematurely and closed the lens whilst the ball was still floating downward. The white glowing object was in view for just two or three seconds.

Although the witness could not recall the date when the picture was taken, reconstruction based on the weather records suggests to Alex Keul that it was 3 or 4 August 1978. The slide itself shows a curved trail of bright light with a ball at the end, casting sparks as it falls across the frame. It superficially resembles a flare or firework rocket, which was the source of one of the first investigation options.

On this theory, Claus Feuerstein, an expert with a fireworks manufacturers in Salzburg, studied the picture and noted that it had features 'completely unusual with firework objects'. He cited several key reasons why the explanation did not fit.

Dr Zdenek Ceplecha, a Czechoslovakian astronomer specializing in meteors, ruled them out but showed how the optics suggested this was a real object descending by gravity. He thought it might be a firework.

Other analysis checked the object against more mundane lightning activity. But of most interest was an attempt to conduct computer enhancement, as has been applied to UFO photographs in the recent past. Here a computer turns the photo into electrical signals, then enhances any aspect of it so as to bring out fine details, finally producing a new, improved print. The process was successfully developed during the 1970s by NASA for their deep space probes where cameras could not return from space. In place of film brought back from Mars or Jupiter only electrical signals could be beamed across millions of miles.

Dr Peter Marx, an image processing specialist at UCLA in Los Angeles, did some work on this ball lightning case and found something akin to atmospheric turbulence surrounding the descending ball. This suggests it was a real object with an actual mass that was displacing the air as it passed through, not an optical effect of some sort.

A lively debate followed throughout 1992 in the pages of *J. Met* with assorted suggestions about possible meteors creating ionization trails as they sped through the atmosphere. However, the matter remains unresolved and the Vorarlberg photograph may yet turn out to be useful evidence for this little-understood phenomenon.

Not everyone is as impressed by the evidence for ball lightning as this. Steuart Campbell, who once used it as a prime explanation for UFO reports, wrote a major thesis on the subject for the *Skeptic*, a magazine which is published by a team of scientists who seek to argue for rationality as opposed to the paranormal.

'The existence of ball lightning is not certain,' he reports, adding, 'it is important to point out that [this existence] is an *assumption*.' He suggests that researchers are often reluctant to consider the 'null hypothesis' (ie that what they seek may not exist) and so the evidence tends to become distorted.

He offers several possible solutions to cases, many of which he claims to have found by analysis. These include optical illusions, focusing problems with cameras and, a novel concept, the idea that ball lightning reports may sometimes be refracted mirages created by bright stars or planets at or just below earth's horizon. He cites Venus and the star Antares in two cases that he has looked into.

Whilst insisting that he is not claiming that ball lightning does not exist, merely advocating that the option be taken seriously, he notes that the constant failure either to find hard evidence or to come up with a theory that makes sense of the many divergent reports can be 'explained most simply by proposing that ball lightning does not exist.'

On 11 July 1992 Steuart Campbell proposed these challenging views at a conference on ball lightning that was staged at Oxford Polytechnic. Perhaps he will repeat them in September 1993 at a European congress on the subject, being organized, with delicious forethought that science so rarely practises, in the same Montafon Valley of Austria where that hot potato of a photographic case took place fifteen years before!

The Fatima Miracle

Steuart Campbell is nothing if not versatile. During 1992 he was writing a book applying his unique mirage theory to some of the world's most famous UFO reports. At the same time the Scottish mysteries journal *Enigmas* (November 1992) featured his analysis of the visions at Fatima in Portugal. These form one of the classic cases of supernatural lore.

For six months during 1917 three Catholic children claimed to have seen 'the Virgin' in a grotto and had various regular conversations with her. These resulted in famous 'prophecies' which have only ever been revealed after the events supposedly presaged in them have come to pass. The first was said to describe Communism, the next World War II and another – reputedly held unopened by the Vatican in Rome – assorted horrible dooms for the last few years of the twentieth century. Periodically campaigns are mounted to urge the pontiff to reveal this last great secret to the world and legends abound that this has not been done because it speaks of the fall of the papacy itself.

During the later Virgin 'encounters' groups of visitors watched and prayed at the grotto during the visions, although they never seem to have seen the Virgin themselves. As the fame of the children spread, so did the number of spectators. Finally it was announced that the last visit would be on 13 October 1917 and a great event was anticipated on that date.

It is estimated that up to 100,000 people were attracted by the grapevine to attend and so either witness, or scoff at, whatever did, or more probably did not, take place. The fact is that, according to eyewitnesses and at least one (very poor) photograph, a miracle did indeed occur. Supposedly the sun dulled and then descended from the sky to fly around the crowd as a ball of light.

Across the years a number of paranormal interpretations have been placed upon these supposed events, which seem to be sufficiently well attested by witnesses to make it certain that something happened. One convoluted theory attempts to show that the Virgin was really an alien and that the 'sun' seen by this vast crowd was in fact her spaceship. Other weird ideas are summarized well in David Barclay's privately published book '*Fatima: a close encounter of the worst kind*'.

Most eyewitness accounts tell how the morning was dull but the rain cleared before noon. The sun, to which one child pointed, was easy to look at through a thin veil of cloud, which was then thrust apart to 'whirl and turn' in a circle. People fell to the ground and were bathed in shafts of light pouring from this hole ripped in the cloud.

One witness said that the sun took on the appearance of a 'glazed wheel made of mother-of-pearl' and then fell from the sky spinning wildly and making the atmosphere turn reddish-purple. There were reports of unusual solar effects being temporarily seen from other parts of Portugal on that same day.

Various ideas were suggested, such as fog or mist surrounding the sun, but it was certainly established that this was not any normally predictable event such as an eclipse.

Steuart Campbell, however, believes he has found a meteorological solution. He argues that a cloud of dust passing across the face of the sun made it possible to look directly upon it, then created the colour changes and optical illusions of it spinning, advancing and retreating.

He looked for the source of a dust cloud but the weather records offered little support for the idea that it was raised from the Sahara desert. I recall during my schooldays in the mid 1960s one such cloud literally blocking out the sun so completely that day was turned virtually into night in Manchester, causing not a few to panic about the end of the world. Next day cars were covered in layers of thick red Sahara sand. If this sand was not the origin of the Fatima dust, Campbell suggests that a volcanic eruption, perhaps weeks or months before, spewed debris into the upper atmosphere. But he was unable to find a clear candidate.

Margaret Fry, a paranormal researcher from North Wales, investigated a remarkable case of a Fatima rerun on 4 October 1986. This was in the Prestatyn/Rhyl coastal area. Several witnesses in mid afternoon reported a round white shape, a reddish halo effect, spinning and rotating patterns and other phenomena. They took a series of photographs of these – some of which I purchased from them. Although they were initially adamant that they cannot have seen the sun because it was possible to look directly at the white ball (just as witnesses at Fatima had said) and also because there was no cloud in the sky to mask its face, they undoubtedly did photograph this. However, it is equally certain that they filmed the sun by way of an unusual high layer of ice particles or mist which caused a filtering and distortion. The result was the rotations, colour changes and other effects which the sequence of photographs depict.

In my mind this 'miracle of Prestatyn' is remarkably akin to whatever took place at Fatima sixty-nine years to the month before. But that diagnosis by itself is not without problems. Overlooked in such analysis is the undeniable and quite bizarre coincidence as to why at Fatima, if Steuart Campbell is correct, this exceptionally rare chance atmospheric event should occur at precisely the time and date of the pre-planned visit and the expected miracle. This was after all why the big crowd was drawn there in the first place.

Science may indeed have found a possible solution to the mechanics of this incident, but it is a solution that poses many new questions.

The Martian Face

Earth has its pyramids, stone circles and sphinxes. We might wonder just how visible these would be from any spaceship orbiting the globe, probing us to seek out new life-forms. Would they suggest to others the presence of intelligence on this planet? Are they sufficient to show that more than natural forces were at work?

During 1992 a contentious issue surrounded the launch of a new unmanned spaceflight to Mars. Launched in September, it will start beaming back, from orbit late in 1993, pictures which will have a remarkable degree of resolution. They will probably be good enough to answer what may be the red planet's greatest secret. But will NASA even try, and if not, why not?

Mars seems to have its own version of the Sphinx and pyramids; something that – if established as fact – will once and for all settle those long arguments about whether we are lonely rulers of the universe. If proved real we would have 'brothers' on Mars or at least they would have once existed at some point in the distant past.

The cause of the controversy is some photographs taken by a previous orbiting mission which had photographed the Martian surface in intense detail in 1976. These images depict the Cydonia region of the northern desert, with its high mountains, ridges and valleys. Geologists believe that some Martian valleys may show signs that they were formed by running water. If so it disappeared from the planet's surface aeons ago – but may have been the basis for some type of life way back in our prehistory, before Mars lost its atmosphere and effectively died.

However, in addition to these mundane geological features there are several real anomalies in a tract of land about the size of London or Chicago. They include a five-sided pyramid shape, but the most dramatic of all is what appears to be a one-mile-wide humanoid face carved out of rock. It stares back at us across the darkness of space to challenge all our concepts about the unique, supreme status of human intelligence.

Is this Martian face real, or just an illusion; a trick of light, shade and shadow? If real, who put it there, and when? Scientists seem to be reluctant to mount a mission that would answer these questions once and for all. NASA have for some time dismissed the matter as just a chance quirk, not a real phenomenon of importance. Until 1992 they seemed determined not to rephotograph that part of the Martian surface.

Yet this is an intriguing scientific puzzle which instantly captures attention. It could help sell a mission to Mars to cost-conscious budget controllers and support other research on the flight. If sent, such a mission could settle the disputes easily and quickly. But there has been no promise that this will be done even now.

A number of prominent people have come out in support of the so-called 'monuments of Cydonia' and forced something of a rethink. It is at last possible we may get an answer soon. Ex NASA astronaut and physicist Dr Brian O'Leary, who actually trained for manned missions to Mars before budget cuts scrapped them, is one such supporter. I worked with him in Australia recently and was very impressed with his forthright perspective on this matter. He told me that he was at first a sceptic, believing NASA's 'trick of the light' solution, but was convinced by the hard work put in by a group of experts, notably Richard Hoagland, a computer specialist from California.

Hoagland researched images that had been dug up by Vincent DiPietro and Gregory Molenaar. Some 60,000 camera shots were checked and turned up a vital clue. The 'face' was present on different days when the cameras mapped this precise part of the surface terrain from different angles. This made the light and shade theory much more difficult to argue with any conviction. Similarly, enhancement of the images, rather than decreasing the resemblance to a face, as it ought to have done if this was merely an illusion triggered by a chance relationship, actually increased it. The computer brought out details that look like eyeballs, for example.

Since then Hoagland has made further extraordinary claims. He says that he has traced a mathematical relationship between the monuments and he and colleagues note a pattern linking them with structures on earth (eg Silbury Hill in Wiltshire!) This, coupled with the very human visage of the 'Martian' in the face has led to an expression of more disquiet than the indisputable puzzle of the pictures themselves.

However, the 'Mars Mission', a project Hoagland coordinates, has answers to these problems. It is suggested, for example, that the image is deliberately human and was put there, not by indigenous Martians, but by space travellers who visited both Mars and Earth millenia ago. Rather like the famous black monolith in Arthur C. Clarke's seminal story of extra-terrestrial contact (*2001: A Space Odyssey*) the purpose was for us to see it, and thereby know that we are not alone, when we reached the correct level of technological development. In other words it was a kind of calling card from ET – or even a Martian equivalent of someone scrawling 'Kilroy was here' on a wall!

In February 1992 Dr Hoagland was invited to present his findings to a gathering at the United Nations in New York. Such was the level of interest that two separate presentations had to be staged. There are already signs that his evidence has had some influence. I met a NASA researcher at a conference in the USA three months later and he told me some heads were spinning with the possibilities; indeed that, but for the fall of communism that has created economic chaos in the former USSR, a joint NASA and Soviet flight to Mars to resolve the mystery could have been under way by now. Even so it may only be a matter of time before we find out once and for all whether the Martian deserts really do have an alien sculpture on them.

The Hum

One of the least known yet most baffling mysteries of the modern world reached epidemic proportions during 1992. The humadruzz came back with a vengeance to attack communities on both sides of the Atlantic.

Humadruzz is an uncomfortable name coined many years ago for a mysterious sound that people claim to hear, most commonly in the middle of the night. The word is onomatopoeic, describing the noise it is meant to convey – a sound which is a cross between a low-level buzzing, humming and droning. Victims describe it as just below the hearing threshold of many people and with a frequency of about 16 hertz.

When there is a new outbreak it is presumed to be a one-off local incident and discussed in that context, but the hum is a long-term problem that has plagued developed countries at least since 1958, according to my files. This must be important to any attempt to understand what it is.

In the early days a number of strange ideas were trotted out, such as that creatures living beneath the earth were tunnelling at night. UFOs, of course, often got the blame, even though commonly nothing is seen. More sensible theories involved mining machinery, newly invented jet engines bouncing off cloud and even wind through new-fangled television aerials!

The passage of time has shown these theories to be a nonsense. But eventually science minister Lord Hailsham, acting for the British government, launched an inquiry. That was in 1960. Although the National Physics Laboratory offered support, nothing came of it. Victims of the hum were locked in soundproofed rooms and still said they heard it – even though others nearby could not. There were reports of people being forced to move, several alleged nervous breakdowns caused by the perpetual noise and there was one unproven claim of suicide triggered by the phenomenon.

I first investigated a case of the hum in October 1966 in Manchester, where a professional dancer reported that it was keeping her awake at night and sounded like 'electricity gone mad'.

The idea was proposed that the hum resulted from an ear infection which caused the sounds to be generated internally. Only those with the problem heard it, because nothing was really there. This failed to persuade witnesses but the subject disappeared from regular discussion and only a few researchers continued to monitor the activity. We knew from such work that this was not a problem that was about to go away. I have maintained my interest because I too have regularly heard the hum!

So we come to 1992, when new outbreaks occurred and, predictably enough, were assumed to be the first and only times the sound had ever haunted a local community.

In January 1992 the hum struck Hueytown in Alabama. It was alleged to keep people awake, start dogs howling and create problems through teeth vibrations. Victims who suffered it for weeks on end reported that wet nights were the worst and that it did seem most severe in the early hours, both common factors in reports from Britain in the 1960s.

Because Hueytown was a mining area there was a popular local theory that fans in the mine shafts might be to blame. The company argued against this, saying that they were not using fans any different from those installed in 1974 and that there had been no previous complaints. The critics fought back by showing that a forest between the mines and Hueytown was felled during 1991, thus changing the conditions. A planning officer pointed out that he had once seen how a freak combination of air pressure, humidity, temperature and ground terrain could create a kind of local echo chamber and channel noise from military exercises across seventeen miles of Maryland countryside to where it then disturbed a small town.

However, as has been the case everywhere else, the Hueytown hum (temporarily, at least) subsided in early 1992 and the story was forgotten. But it is safe to predict it is not yet over.

Whilst the people of this American town were wrestling with what was to them a unique dilemma I was involved in an ongoing debate about almost identical 'soundings' in Gloucestershire, England. There were certainly no coal-mine fans responsible for this hum. But, as is often the case, a local scapegoat was branded.

The most affected zone was around the smart suburban areas of Cheltenham and Stroud. The low-frequency sound had begun at almost exactly the same time that it started thousands of miles away in Hueytown (early December 1991) and had continued night and day, but mostly night, becoming intense during January 1992. As I can attest, you notice it most when you waken in the night, a time when most other sounds are suppressed.

A witness from Chipping Campden reported how 'because of their low-frequency nature, the sounds are very penetrating,' noting that the inside of a house acts like an amplifier. In other cases the hum was said to produce physiological effects, notably tiredness, headaches and skin tingling. Several migraine sufferers (myself included) suspect it is a part of their problem.

I have felt for some time that low-frequency electromagnetic radiation might be the source. Some theories link the Gloucestershire sound with GCHQ, a spy and electronic telecommunications centre near Stroud. This suggestion was, of course, rejected.

I think there are increasing grounds to believe that the phenomenon may result from electromagnetic pollution which has risen steadily from the mid 1950s onwards. A series of microwave energy repeater towers are beaming invisible radiation around the country and there is some scientific research to link the hum with this. I suspect that what is happening is that the radiation is turned into auditory signals (and other physical symptoms) by some people, such as those with sensitive tissue in their brain cortex. As a result they literally absorb and decode this raw energy that to many people is simply inaudible and undetectable. But there is more to it than that. I hope to publish a detailed report later linking hypothetical environmental pollution with some mysterious electrical disturbances and various 'paranormal' phenomena.

On 14 January 1992 I published some of my thoughts in an article in the *Gloucestershire Echo* in order to alert local residents pestered by the hum. The idea was to ensure that they knew they were not alone in their experience, but also to obtain reports of the outbreak, which, as I predicted, began to fade away in February and become less of a nuisance than it was. From experience I must say that this is at least partially because victims become accustomed to the noise and so filter it out of their consciousness, just as chronic sufferers of pain can learn to live with this. I do not believe the problem of the hum is going to disappear.

My ideas did pique the interest of Alan Taylor, chief environmental health officer for Cheltenham. He felt that microwaves, being higher in frequency than that claimed for the auditory level of the hum, may not be responsible, but agreed the concept was 'interesting' and should not be discounted. But the low frequency hum is just an aspect of a wider range of problems covering a broad frequency spectrum. Microwave energy is probably only part of the answer. In any case, what the brain thinks it hears is not, of course, an actual sound but a simulation triggered by the absorption of the energy. This need not be directly related to the frequency of the electromagnetic radiation that may be washing around.

In March 1992 it was decided that a new government enquiry would be launched, some thirty-two years after Lord Hailsham's. £50,000 was allocated by the Department of the Environment and an open-minded study was promised. To date, and so far as I can ascertain, there has been no attempt to check out the electromagnetic radiation theory.

It has focused instead on two other solutions – that there is a hearing defect common to the witnesses or that new high-pressure underground gas pipes ten feet below the surface are to blame. As these have only been fitted from 1966 onward and only since 1970 in any numbers, this last idea (which the Gas Board has also investigated and refuted) was for me a non-starter right away. Unfortunately, few realize the extent of the evidence for the hum well before such pipes were fitted. Once they do, that alone destroys all possibility that they are the cause. But the enquiry has already proven useful, in ruling out the 'hearing defect' theory with its checks on twenty-five victims.

The Building Research Establishment at Watford is making further study. The Department of the Environment in London also confirmed in 1992 some news which may astonish you. It receives 500 reports each year from people complaining about the mystery hum. To put this into perspective, that number is greater than the sightings of UFOs that are made to the Ministry of Defence during most years. So you can imagine how many cases are not reported publicly. UFOs, of course, are a world-renowned phenomenon. The hum is almost unknown other than to its victims.

Hopefully the events of 1992 have made more people aware that there is a problem to be addressed, and cases of witnesses who get a buzz in their bedrooms late at night will be recorded by more researchers into anomalous phenomena. I would be pleased to hear about them.

There has also been some intriguing parallel research reported in *J. Met* during the year. It suggests from anecdotal accounts culled from the meteorological records that aerial hummings might have occurred on a more sporadic basis through history. Whilst the meteorologists are seeking out theories to account for this fact, I suspect such a finding may relate to naturally emitted electromagnetic radiation. This could have a similar effect on the brain tissue to the artificial variety we are playing with today. There are simply more cases of the hum now because we have boosted the amount of this bath of radiated energy through our activities within the airwaves.

When my subsequent report about the hum is published, I hope to show that some modern-day 'paranormal' happenings have been occurring in greater numbers alongside the rise in intensity of this sound because both are by-products of the same triggering phenomenon. We have for some years now rather carelessly polluted our atmosphere with the intangible and not very politically sensitive toxicant of electromagnetic radiation. Increasing numbers of people are perhaps beginning to reap the resultant whirlwind.

Crop Circles

1992 was the year that the crop circle mystery died. At least, that is how many people see the situation. After being at the forefront of popular attention for several summers, attracting interest (it is said) from presidents, prime ministers and even royalty, suddenly the bubble burst and those who were believers found themselves almost isolated.

There were more than 500 newspaper stories about crop circles in Britain alone during the summer months of both 1990 and 1991. Between April and October 1992 there were less than 150. What provoked such a dramatic decrease in attention? did it reflect the end of a phenomenon?

If there is anybody who does not know what a crop circle is by now, a brief introduction will suffice. In July 1989 paranormal investigators Colin Andrews and Pat Delgado published a book called *Circular Evidence*, full of aerial pictures of mysterious swirled circles gouged into cereal fields across Hampshire and Wiltshire. It was a wonderful mystery, they announced, speculating about unknown energy fields manipulated by unknown intelligences. Their book captured the imagination of the world and suddenly millions of people started talking crop circles. Organizations were founded. Magazines were launched. Overnight this had become the great toy of the New Age community. It was a perfect combination of space age speculation, mysticism and tangible evidence undeniably there for all to see.

Unfortunately, there were a few things not well known amidst the furore. Circles were neither a new phenomenon nor confined to southern England. They had been appearing all over the world for quite a long time and cases as far back as 1590 are known. Modern investigation had indeed begun in Wiltshire when several were found near Westbury in 1980 and there had been steady media publicity ever since. But despite the claims that this was a deep-rooted mystery, a working hypothesis linked with spinning vortices of electrified air had been gradually developed by meteorologists studying the circles. They, at least, insisted that this was not a supernatural mystery, just a little-known wonder of nature.

Inevitably, the massive public attention suddenly focused on the subject after the runaway success of *Circular Evidence* coaxed jokers out of the woodwork. The British UFO Research Association (BUFORA), for which I coordinate field investigations, had been studying the circles from that 1980 appearance onward, if only to establish that they were not the landing marks of spaceships (as the tabloid papers quickly suggested). As early as July 1983 the first hoax was detected by UFOlogists, when one national newspaper tried to fool another into accepting a complex series of circles it had paid to create. The other paper ignored it, so nothing was said until the truth was established by investigators and an admission squeezed out.

This was not to be the last time trickery would descend upon the cornfields. But of course the idea that these strange marks were a combination of 'human engineering' (the polite term circle investigators use for hoaxing!) and unusual types of electrified air was hardly something to set the world on fire. The more sensational theories, from aliens to mystic forces, were what the media needed. So the fact that hoaxing was taking place tended to be ignored by many journalists, and the growing breed of crop circle researchers (or 'cereologists' as they named themselves) often put it out of mind just as easily.

Little sign that the penny was dropping seems to have been apparent even when there was a dramatic escalation in circle numbers (from about fifty a summer to about three or four hundred in the two years after the publication of Andrews and Delgado's book.) Even more worrying was that the circles suddenly changed in character to become complex formations of lines and curves, and with a decidedly symbolic nature. These were so obviously artificial that those who proposed a meteorological solution appeared to be defeated by the new twists. The phenomenon had responded to show the world the truth. These new circle types (named 'pictograms' by the researchers) simply could not be anything other than the product of an intelligence. They were far too artificial to be produced by nature.

Unfortunately, too few people realized that there is a type of intelligence which does not reside on Venus or in some other dimension. It is one that has two arms, two legs and absolutely revels in the thought of getting one up on mystic believers or scientists who say that they can explain everything in sobering terms. We call these creatures human beings and with crop circles they were in their element.

In September 1991, at the end of that year's hectic and spectacularly picturesque season, two retired artists, Doug Bower and Dave Chorley (usually known affectionately as Doug and Dave), went to the tabloid newspaper *Today* to claim that they had faked up to a couple of hundred of the best circles during more than a decade of japery, including those original pictograms that had appeared soon after Andrews and Delgado's book. They were, in effect, responsible for the variety of the circle phenomenon as it appeared in late 1991, although often it was mis-implied that they had fabricated *all*, or even most, of the crop circles. This is something they have never claimed to have done. At the most they say they made about 10 per cent of those that had been found in southern England since 1980 and perhaps 6 or 7 per cent of those which had appeared around the world.

Today did not take them at their word. They set up an experiment. The amiable pair faked a pictogram in Kent and then hid whilst Pat Delgado was brought to examine it. The circle researcher was cited by the journalists as being highly impressed and pronouncing it genuine. Then, a couple of days later, they broke the sad news. He had been fooled by a Doug and Dave creation, and if he had been taken in on this occasion then the same thing may well have happened many times before. Doug and Dave seemed to be vindicated. They even pointed to the fact that they had 'signed' the last few of their circles after making the decision that they would 'retire' after the harvesting of their final year's efforts. Sure enough the photographs of some of those late summer 1991 patterns do display the unmistakable trace of two letter Ds etched into the crop. These, the men say, are D for Doug and D for Dave.

At first Pat Delgado was quoted as accepting that the game was up. But he later reassessed the situation and seemed to smell a rat. He was by no means the only one to do that. Most of the cereology movement stuck firmly to the view that all was not lost after all, whatever Doug and Dave might say.

However Dr Terence Meaden, the physicist whose ionized air vortex theory had been the great white hope of rational science, was also ensnared by a team of hoaxers from a sceptics group late that summer. This further revelation hit the community with a devastating blow. If neither Meaden nor Delgado could be relied upon to spot a hoax, then who on earth could? It was at least now defensible that there never had been a crop circle phenomenon but that every case from the very start was simply a hoax, sometimes by Doug and Dave but also by various assorted copycat groups with a variety of motivations.

As 1992 began the entire crop circle community was reeling from shell-shock. Was there anything to salvage amidst the ruins of a phenomenon or had the entire subject been destroyed by such trickery?

The 1992 circle season

1992 was to be a disappointing summer, in terms both of weather and of its crop of British circles. Far fewer were recorded outside Britain than in previous years and over 95 per cent of the 200 or so that appeared within Britain came from one area in Wiltshire (with few even in Hampshire). The non-Wessex percentage was substantially down on previous years.

Perhaps the Doug and Dave story had reduced the level of interest overall and limited the widespread hoaxing that I certainly believe was behind a large fraction of circle cases worldwide throughout 1989, 1990 and 1991. After all, once the media lost interest there may have seemed little point in isolated jokers creating small circles that could not hope to emulate the beauty or the publicity that had become attached to Doug and Dave's creative catalogue.

But some hoaxing certainly did go on during 1992. Indeed many researchers were visibly shaken by the extent to which it appeared to dominate the scene. Perhaps partly as a defence mechanism against previous excesses they tended to take the cautious line and pronounce any circle as possibly hoaxed rather than run the risk of being trapped again. Undoubtedly there were those who still had motives to fake circles and several such groups became apparent during the year. For example, agricultural college students fought a friendly war with rivals to see who could create the best formations!

Elsewhere, the tourist appeal of the circles was not to be overlooked. Occasional farmers still charged entrance fees to see strange shapes that appeared on their land. Formations cropped up right next to pubs where, real or not, they were an undoubted boon. A tour company flew parties of circle hunters across the Atlantic, notably from Kansas, on a venture probably planned before the demise of the phenomenon became quite so obvious. They employed cereologists to show the punters around whatever sites were in evidence by mid summer.

Nothing significantly new appeared, although August did bring a handful of complex pictograms. The most memorable pattern was a giant snail etched into a field at Alton Barnes. Here a farmer has had a caravan for several summers to give entrance to those people who still want to study these amazing shapes at close hand. Another ringed circle appeared right next to Silbury Hill and a small pictogram on a hill directly overlooking the Avebury stone circle. These associations with the earth mystery sites of the area were prominent and local shops now sell modern-day circle memorabilia almost as avidly as they do postcards, mugs and T-shirts about these wonders of the ancient British landscape.

The first circle of the year appeared at Sutton Scotney in rape seed on 28 April but the small formation was rough, placed right by the main road and easily reached by the first tractor line into the field (the method hoaxers use to avoid leaving tell-tale footprints). As such it was almost universally labelled a fraud.

The crop circle magazines featured 1992 patterns far less than in previous years, concentrating instead on seeking out other types of evidence or retrospective assessments of what are viewed as important cases.

At the end of the year Paul Fuller published a map showing the locations of twenty groups of hoaxers he believed were responsible for creating at least a handful of circles each. This information was collated from the active team of tireless correspondents to his *Crop Watcher* magazine. It created some controversy, but was only a more structured version of what many others were privately suggesting. Even in the main crop circle conferences during July and August news of 'insider' hoaxers, given pseudonyms like 'Bill Bailey' and 'Spiderman' by cereologist George Wingfield, were taking up time.

An American journalist, Jim Schnabel, who was writing a book about circles and who had upset some parts of the cereology community with his uncompromising approach towards hoaxing, exposed a new long-term team of adventurers in an article written with colleague Rob Irving for the *Independent Magazine* (29 August).

This team of three or four youths, which he named as the UBI (United Bureau of Investigation) had created dozens of circles and were based in Wiltshire. One of their favourite tricks, they told the journalists, was to touch up already existing circles and add features that made them appear more artificial. Paul Fuller claimed that some hoaxers did this because they saw this as a way towards possible 'alien' communication.

Fuller also wrote in *Crop Watcher* (September 1992) that he believed video evidence had been obtained of UBI activities and that in 1991 the team had even kept a close watch on meteorologists with the CERES team in the presumed hope of scuppering a monitor operation they were secretly conducting, perhaps by the creation of fake circles right under the noses of the scientists.

Either way, the revelations about another group of long-term hoaxers only added to the view that there must be others who had yet to be fully exposed as key factors in the circle game. The true extent of trickery within the phenomenon was being seriously underemphasized.

The research

As 1992 began some optimism was attached to startling test results that had just been reported from late 1991 crop circles. They had been produced by Michael Chorost, working with the American UFO group, MUFON. He had visited Britain and taken soil samples from just five of the complex formations that had formed that year, at least one a widely accepted hoax. Control soil from outside each circle was also taken. These were then all flown back to the USA and tested by Marshall Dudley, an engineer in Oak Ridge, Tennessee. Highly sensitive gas flow counters were used to determine the alpha and beta radiation from the samples.

Preliminary results seemed to suggest that there were ionizing radiation anomalies and other tests elsewhere on the cell structure of plants in the circles were also said to indicate that this radiation might have altered their genetic composition in some way.

In the immediate wake of Doug and Dave this was news too good to keep quiet. It was a powerful antidote to the now widespread view that the circle mystery was all a hoax. Two artists using wooden boards and a length of rope could hardly have produced such major changes in the crop, if these results were valid. Something far more puzzling had to be occurring.

A debate ensued within the *Crop Watcher* with editor Paul Fuller, a professional statistician, challenging the validity of the methodology that had been used (January 1992) and Michael Chorost (from Duke University) responding (May 1992). Although they disagreed over some points, a consensus was reached that the tests as conducted in 1991 had major flaws and that the inconclusive and contentious nature of the outcome indicated that further and better work was needed.

The 1991 results were thus put on the back burner by the spring and meanwhile Chorost and colleagues rounded up major grant funding to the tune of several thousand dollars to mount a new experiment in England during the summer months of 1992. This was to be named Project Argus. It would run from mid July to late August. Argus would tighten up many of the procedures. Paul Fuller met with Dr Ernie Peck (dean of science and maths at the University of Nevada) and Dr Trevor Pinch (a sociologist from Cornell), both over with the Argus team to take part in the much enhanced operation. He confirmed (*Crop Watcher*, July 1992) that 'I have to say that I could not fault the team's attitude towards its task. Neither could I fault the team's sampling techniques or methodology.'

Argus took ten samples and ten controls from every circle in one county (Wiltshire) which had appeared after they set up operations and to which they could gain rapid access. That meant about forty-five cases. This overcame some difficulties which are due to fluctuations in normal background radiation count across larger swathes of land, and, as a further precaution against contamination, readings of emissions were taken in Britain itself and then flown to five different universities in the USA. At these locations each team worked on results 'blind', having no idea what sites they came from or even if they were real or control samples. A wide range of circle types were surveyed, including some fakes where hoaxers were actually observed making the circles in question!

Argus was by far the best funded and the most thorough and carefully planned scientific analysis of the crop circles to date and if anything could establish evidence of the much heralded radiation contamination or frequently alleged changes in plant cell structure this was it. As of early 1993 detailed results have yet to be announced, perhaps symptomatic of the caution that is now wisely filling the crop circle world. However, those who were involved seem to suggest that there are unlikely to be any startling revelations.

Ralph Noyes, one of the founders of the Centre for Crop Circle Studies (CCCS) and a former official in the Ministry of Defence, gave a preliminary view based on his personal involvement in the Argus work (the *Circular*, October 1992). He noted that no 'litmus test' to detect real from fake circles had emerged from the study. Extensive experiments were applied to measure many types of emission, including static and magnetic fields, and it may prove necessary to design special equipment to try to measure any changes that may be occurring which seem to be at a far smaller concentration than previously expected (ie parts per million rather than per thousand). Also the suggestions of ionizing radiation hinted at from the 1991 results appear not to have been vindicated and Noyes suggests that the circles may owe more to what he termed 'non ionizing radiation at some point or points in the electromagnetic spectrum'. If so, this would be a blow to meteorologists like Dr Meaden, who have argued in favour of a rotating vortex of ionized air.

It remains to be seen if further scientific support and funding can be mounted to continue the promising start that Argus has made. It will also be interesting to see how the results from unresolved 1992 circles compare with any from known (or strongly suspected) hoaxes during the time when the project operated. If fake circles do not show radically different results from those obtained from circles without suspicion of trickery then the possibility that there were no real circles at all formed during 1992 would have to be taken very seriously. That could prove a mortal wound for the field of cereology.

Hoaxing to order

The only crop circle event of 1992 to achieve substantial publicity was also the most controversial. It was a competition, with big money prizes, challenging people to fake pictograms. Superficially this seems like a sensible (if rather belated) idea in the wake of Doug and Dave's claims. It must make sense to test how easy it is to fabricate circles. Of course, some researchers knew even before the two artists made their claims that hoaxing was going on. My own circle studies in northern Britain had by 1992 ruled two-thirds of cases to be fake. But a number of key researchers staked reputations on the claim that hoaxing was at worst a minor irritation, so they needed to react to the sad truth now forcefully brought home to them.

It was no doubt hoped by some that any circles created in this competition would be poor in comparison with the real thing and that it could be shown how human beings simply could not manufacture the precision, beauty or complexity of form that was appearing in the crop fields. However, if such a hope existed, it was to be dashed.

The competition was not welcomed by all cereologists, but this had little to do with its possible outcome, one way or another, nor indeed its undeniably useful aim to gauge what hoaxing could achieve. Rather the reservations stemmed from potential repercussions on the farming community of what was effectively giving a licence to hoaxers. The best practised tricksters would receive large financial recompense.

Although the location of the competition itself (a field in Buckinghamshire) was carefully selected and kept secret to all bar the entrants and organizers, this was never the real problem. That stemmed from the fact that the £5000 total prize money was given prominent international publicity weeks beforehand and so the many would-be hoaxers had months of virgin crop fields to practise their artistry upon before the great day arrived. It was, of course, utterly predictable that some of those who planned to make a serious effort to win the prize were going to inadvertently wreak havoc in farmers' fields in order to prepare their efforts for the big event. Indeed some entrants later admitted they did exactly that.

However valuable the competition might turn out to be, I therefore felt personally that it was unintentionally offering a green light to a form of organized vandalism and that we simply did not have the right to impose this on a farming community already hit by the recession. Whilst circles themselves rarely destroy cops, gawping sightseers crashing into fields to study the patterns are not so harmless. Some farmers were losing hundreds of thousands of pounds this way. Because of this, I decided not to back the experiment and spoke out against it, although my letter expressing my reasons was, rather unsurprisingly, ignored.

I was not alone in these misgivings. Paul Fuller came out against the competition in *Crop Watcher* and some of the pioneers of circles research and its best known writers, from both the scientific and 'unknown intelligence' schools of thought, also declined support.

The competition, staged on 12 July, had some surprising names behind it. Involvement from the *Cerealogist* magazine and some participation by CCCS members was not unexpected. More so was the pivotal role of the *Guardian* newspaper. In July 1986 they had done BUFORA proud by being one of the first media sources to devote a serious article to our then unheard of 'heresy' that circles were a result of weather effects and hoaxing. Now they acted as the collation point for entries and launched it officially in an article on 8 May. Backing also came from Dr Rupert Sheldrake, a scientist whose revolutionary theories about 'morphic resonance' in his book *A New Science of Life* had once led *Nature* magazine to suggest it was a latter-day candidate for burning!

Sheldrake's interesting theories do suggest a mechanism by which strange phenomena can occur as a sort of 'habit pattern' within belief systems or physical reality. They have stimulated several valuable and unusual experiments in the past. But, whilst I can certainly sympathize with why the biologist felt this hoax experiment might relate to his research, and why, as a scientist, the testing of such a concept was an important step to take, I still doubt the basic wisdom of the idea.

Robin Allen, a noted debunking commentator, wrote of the test in the *Skeptic* magazine and thought it little more than a public relations trick by disgruntled cereologists smarting from the Doug and Dave débâcle. I do not entirely share such cynicism. I suspect the motives of those involved were more honourable even if, in my view, misguided. Nevertheless Allen, who is part of a team called the 'Wessex Skeptics' who have in the past faked circles (including the one that entrapped Dr Terence Meaden and noted circle photographer 'Busty' Taylor during 1991), declined to participate in the competition. Interestingly, Doug and Dave also resisted calls that they should prove their skills.

Only a few days before the entrants took to the fields they were given the design of a complex pictogram shape that they would have to reproduce. They had the hours of darkness to do this in and were allowed a team of up to five people and whatever equipment they needed. The action was observed from a hill overlooking the field; afterwards several stunned cereologists commented on how such a large band of hoaxers beavering away for hours within a small area generated remarkably little noise or sign of their nocturnal activities.

This was warning number one that the hoax theory was not about to bite the dust. Number two followed swiftly, when daylight revealed that the participants had all produced passable renditions of the new pictogram shape. Some, of course, were better than others, but hardly any looked like a crude fake and several people who were once adamant pro-cereologists were forced to conclude that the two or three best examples were difficult, if not impossible, to distinguish from patterns that they would once have called quite real.

Although the team who won the top prize money were skilled men from British Aerospace, they had never worked together before that night. Their leader had, with different help, practised just once. The winner of the second prize was even more significant. It was debunking American journalist Jim Schnabel, who had produced an excellent version of the pictogram in the alloted time without anybody else's help. He told me that Rupert Sheldrake congratulated him on such an amazing effort which clearly affected the scientists' appraisal of the subject.

Indeed, this competition was undoubtedly such a victory for the hoax theory that it established to the satisfaction of any objective critic how fabricating even complex pictograms was neither impossible nor the province only of large teams of trained people. Rather it appears to be so easy that it must surely have happened on many occasions when cereologists had formerly argued that the resulting shape was simply far too complex to have been made by anything other than mystic forces.

New developments

There were some other more positive steps forward in cereology during 1992.

Long serving UFOlogist Omar Fowler, who organizes a group in Derbyshire, received praise for his efforts at trying to establish the influence of microwave energy in crop fields. Since 1985 Fowler had discovered a common denominator in circles researched all over England. This was the existence of single stems of the crop standing upright in otherwise flattened swathes of barley and wheat. Analysing these stems he traced patterns which included burning, kinks and a single bend at the top. Fowler proposes from this that plasma balls of energy might emit high frequency radiation of a wavelength suggestive of microwave emission and thus produce the consistent kinking of this single stem. He now says that the outstanding question is whether this plasma beam is a 'natural phenomenon' and asks 'who or what is transmitting [it] and for what purpose?'

Another type of energy was hypothesized by a man with a name with a wonderfully 'synchronistic' element. Only a handful of people have published books about crop circles since 1989. One of the best known, of course, is Colin Andrews, who has now been joined by Andrew Collins! Collins, best known for his work as a psychic questor (see page 117), conducted a field study of circles and suggested during 1992 that a mysterious force called orgone energy might be involved. Orgone is a controversial atmospheric force supposedly discovered by Austrian scientist Wilhelm Reich in 1939. His work has largely been ignored, although singer Kate Bush did describe his research and efforts at dispersing clouds in her 1985 hit song 'Cloudbusting'.

Collins told *Psychic News* (25 July) that 'Reich believed [orgone] permeated all living matter, that it is present inside and outside the body.' Indeed he added that it was, in effect, the life force that animated matter and 'sustains consciousness'. Further, that 'bioforms' exist of raw orgone that can interact with human consciousness either on an individual or collective level. In the past we have moulded and shaped this energy into what we interpreted as fairies, demons, spirits, aliens or UFOs. Now bursts of orgone were being attracted towards locations on earth where there was a kind of reservoir, and creating patterns on the ground. As humanity responded to the circles our influence on these bioforms increased and a sort of contact took place, resulting in the intelligent design features evident within the phenomenon.

In *Crop Watcher* (September 1992) Andrew Collins discussed his then new book *The Circlemakers*. He feels that the concept offers a bridge between previously warring factions. On the one hand the idea of a natural energy force creating the circles can mesh well with the work of meteorologists arguing for an atmospheric energy as the primary cause. On the other the interactive consciousness and bioforms he sees involved within the orgone theory can be perhaps be that so far unidentified 'unknown intelligence' that others have insisted upon to explain how the phenomenon seems to react to human thoughts and actions (as, of course, hoaxers would do!). Instead of assuming that one explanation is correct and the other false, possibly both can be melded together by the orgone theory.

For summer 1993 Andrew Collins is planning a series of experiments involving psychics, mystic sites, crop circle locations and other aspects of his theory to see if orgone energy can be harnessed and produce circles of some design. Certainly this will be an intriguing new approach to the subject, although in fact, as you will see later in this report, it may not be as unprecedented as it seems.

From the purely scientific point of view perhaps the most important work was a survey carried out by geography graduate Andrew Hewitt who started his project at Huddersfield Polytechnic as a course exercise. He then took it on from there. Hewitt's final thesis was published in detail by *Crop Watcher* (March and May 1992). The work was a computer based statistical analysis of 2200 British crop circles, from which a number of proven hoaxes were omitted and about thirty more cases withdrawn later when serious doubts arose about their status. Thus, whilst there must still be hoaxes within the database, at least some effort was made to reduce their impact.

Owing to lack of resources Hewitt chose to do his most detailed research on a single year's events for which all data likely ever to be obtained had now been secured. The year chosen was 1990. This included the huge total of 672 cases, although this is a somewhat misleading figure because Hewitt counts individual circles, not events. Thus a pictogram with ten sections is scored as ten separate circles, not just one.

The extent of the filter process for hoaxes can be seen by noting that of these 672 circles only one is for the county of Cheshire. I investigated four other 1990 cases in that county which were excluded from the analysis because I found suspect features. Some of these (a ring at Lower Peover, for example) achieved a lot of newspaper and television publicity and the one case that is included (Preston Brook) achieved no publicity at all.

Thirty-three separate counties recorded circles that summer, but Wiltshire utterly dominated with over 60 per cent. Because there could well be social factors (such as increased public awareness, focusing of circle researchers, concentrations of hoaxers) creating this imbalance, Hewitt drew up separate figures for Wiltshire and the rest of Britain.

Possibly his most significant finding was a very clear indication that circles formed more often in lee slopes of prevailing winds. In Wiltshire, for example, fully one third were on north-eastern aspects of hills, fitting the south-western prevailing winds of the area. The figures for Wiltshire and the rest of the UK (where different prevailing winds occur and different aspects were favoured) were both statistically significant, clearly implying that this was not a chance event but a product of whatever mechanism was creating the circles. Meteorologist Dr Terence Meaden had predicted as long ago as 1982 that circles would form on the lee slope of hills if his theory of an atmospheric vortex was correct.

Another discovery supporting an essentially wind-borne cause for circles was the finding that 27.7 per cent of circles formed on steep slopes as opposed to just 9.4 per cent on flat terrain. Indeed 65 per cent of circles formed on sloping ground geographically classified as steep or intermediary. Meteorologists have long claimed that this is why few circles appear in nearly hill-less counties such as Lincolnshire but are frequent in those with rolling downs and slopes like Wiltshire.

Another important finding of the analysis was that even in 1990, a year dominated by the first appearance of the pictograms, 76.6 per cent of all circles were single events – just one simple, swirled circle. These marks are the ones that have been appearing for centuries (records so far traced back to 1590) and in over thirty-five countries (in *Crop Watcher* for July 1992 Keith Basterfield reported on a dozen such cases from Australia, most predating the first unreported trial hoax that Doug and Dave say they carried out in 1976.)

Paul Fuller, commenting on Hewitt's work, noted two things. Firstly that the media in 1990 (and since) understressed the extent to which the single circles dominate, creating the impression that most crop circles are very complex patterns. They do this presumably because the relatively few complex formations look exciting and single circles are effectively old news. Yet, as Fuller indicates secondly, this emphasis on pictograms in newspaper articles and on television coverage must persuade many hoaxers to fabricate complex shapes rather than simple circles, because they (wrongly) presume this is the predominant form of the phenomenon. Indeed, in preliminary work on the circle data prior to 1990 (the first summer after *Circular Evidence* made the subject a big public issue and so ripe for hoaxing) the proportion of single circles is higher still, being well over 80 per cent.

This must be seen in conjunction with the fact that 130 documented cases exist of historical crop circles reported from before the time when Doug and Dave's long-term hoax was even a twinkle in their eyes. Whatever the phenomenon may or may not be, these 130 cannot be the result of the intervention of these two men. Also we know that almost forty solid examples are on file of eyewitnesses who have seen a crop circle appear, dating from early in this century to the present day. In both these sets of data the effect of hoaxing is probably minimized to a far greater extent than it can be elsewhere. There are some very clear results from this information. Not a single example of a pictogram has been found, either in the historical (pre Doug and Dave) records or in the ever-growing eyewitness accounts. And a staggering 97 per cent of these cases involve the observation of nothing but single circles. To me this offers powerfully suggestive evidence that the only real crop circles are single circles. The rest are made by human engineering.

Disinformation?

The response of the cereology community to the Doug and Dave story was fascinating to observe during 1992. There were some very different extremes of response.

Researcher Peter Williams commented in the *Cerealogist* (Winter 1992) that Doug and Dave had shown that 'the real corn circle experts are the ones who make the circles.' In the same issue, Ken Brown, who has become one of the two artists' strongest champions, went out and sought evidence to confirm their work and found it in the form of footprints underneath the surface crop in some circles. His photographs show this indication that human feet had been walking on the fields as the patterns formed. It is hard to spot but obvious once you find it. Presumably the problem was that too few cereologists swarming around circles in Wessex were even looking for the possibility of trickery with anything more than a cursory glance.

Bob Kingsley now a columnist with the CCCS but the founder of a rational journal called the *Circular*, said in the January 1992 issue that 'the jury is still out', discussing Doug and Dave's story with his usual objectivity. He was, however, prepared to put on record that he did not support what were already growing murmurs about the two artists being somehow used as innocent puppets in some massive government disinformation scheme. Kingsley noted, 'There seems to be no reliable evidence that links Doug and Dave with the government or that shows any connections between said government and any of the MBF companies.'

The MBF affair was a cause taken up by physicist and eager lecturer on circles George Wingfield, whose feud with Terence Meaden had been a long one. Their views were about as different as one could get. It stemmed from a note at the bottom of the *Today* newspaper story which attributed the copyright of the article to 'MBF services' despite indicating that the two men had asked for and received no money (other than bus fares – as they later amusingly remembered when interviewed on television!). So who was this mysterious MBF? Doug and Dave claimed to have no idea but initial enquiries at the paper had suggested it was a press agency who organized the publication of the story.

Research by Wingfield and others then suggested that this

press agency was a strange one, if it existed. A long trek through several companies with MBF initials failed to establish one that was provably it; although Wingfield thought he found one that had done some work for the government. He had already gone on record as stating that during Margaret Thatcher's last months in power at No 10 a ministerial level meeting was held to discuss circles. Wingfield would not reveal his sources but said that the use of disinformation by the Ministry of Defence had allegedly been sanctioned. Consequently, the possibility that Doug and Dave had somehow been utilized without their knowledge to discredit cereology was under debate by some researchers.

My enquiries resulted in my being told that 'MBF services' was an invention. The paper, wishing to stop other tabloids stealing their thunder as they are want to do, made it up and put the copyright sign there to ward off competitiors who without it would have thought it a free story. Indeed I was told that MBF stood for an expression used by a peeved farmer when a circle had appeared on his land. This had amused the journalists because the farmer had said 'not on "my bloody farm!" ' I found the idea of a newspaper wishing to protect its story perfectly acceptable, given my years of involvement with the media, and I told Wingfield this when we met in the USA in May. He said it was only one of many similar, but always different, 'explanations' he had heard. I also have to say that my two direct requests to the editors at *Today* newspaper for a clear statement were not replied to, possibly because they were by then fed up with the rumours that they had served as innocent pawns in a machiavellian government disinformation campaign.

Eventually *Crop Watcher* held a competition asking readers to suggest what they thought MBF stood for, with responses ranging from 'made by fungi' to 'mighty big fraud', neither of which is the truth!

However, the idea that there was more than meets the eye to Doug and Dave's story took hold inside cereology as time went by. George Wingfield himself said in the *Cerealogist* that 'there seems very little doubt ... [there is] a deliberate campaign of disinformation to persuade people that the circles phenomenon is just an illusion.' He added that *Today* were 'unwitting' elements of this. In the same magazine Pat Delgado, the researcher entrapped by *Today* and Doug and Dave, was equally forthright. He spoke of an international 'network of intrigue' and official 'debunking campaign' to 'discredit me and the crop circle subject' and that part of the fear of governments was tied in with the 'significant spiritual connotations' of the mystery.

I should add my own conclusions. I can understand why cereologists see the need to defend their positions in this way. I also think it more than likely that there is some governmental interest in the energy that creates the few genuine crop circles. After all, it could be used either offensively or defensively and they must want to monitor such possibilities. But I find it improbable that some sort of campaign to discredit cereology would need to be mounted since the widely divergent and often silly actions of a few members of the vast army of crop circle researchers needs no help and is quite adept at self destruction.

Equally, I suspect *Today* simply saw a good story and tried to protect their own interests. Also, whilst I have some reservations about how many circles Doug and Dave might have made, I personally have seen enough to satisfy myself that they are key factors behind the appearance of the pictograms and the growth of complexity in recent years. Also I have no need to suppose that they did this for any reason other than those they have stated and really find it hard to imagine how they or the newspaper that told their story could be manipulated in the way implied.

The onus of proof of such extraordinary 'disinformation' claims must lie squarely with the cereologists who propose them. Until such hard evidence has been offered I refuse to go down the conspiracy path which so many investigators of the supernatural have trodden before when things started to go wrong.

Alien Contact?

Perhaps the most remarkable stories arising from 1992 stem from the claims that a form of long-sought alien contact in the cornfields may have become a reality. Whether you see this as a major breakthrough only you can judge from the sincerely offered allegations.

On 22 June BBC television's regional news programme *South Today* carried an interview with noted writer Colin Andrews in which he made some remarkable predictions. He told how a group of scientists (not Argus, it seems) were visiting the next month and that there was a belief that between 20 and 30 July contact would be established with the intelligent force behind the circles. He added that these 'external components', which previously he had not elaborated upon, were what had been loosely termed UFOs in the past.

This was indeed a startling turn of events. One of the pioneers of the field was effectively suggesting that something truly remarkable was on the cards and even giving specific dates. I received calls from several researchers in Wiltshire pleading with me to come down because the whole community 'felt' and 'sensed' that the 'big day' was now imminent. I did indeed visit Wessex and fly over the fields with 'Busty' Taylor but saw and experienced nothing mysterious.

Trying to fathom out the meaning behind this rapidly spreading conviction, it seems that Steven Greer was one of the key figures that Andrews referred to. George Wingfield had already told me of his dealings with this man and evidently Colin Andrews had met him in the USA. Now he was coming to Britain to try his unique 'experiments' in the fields. Greer believed that it was possible to initiate what he called 'close encounters of the fifth kind' by using powerful laser beams to signal into the sky at sensitive sites and that the forces behind UFOs could respond and create encounters. He had most actively tested out this equipment at the town of Gulf Breeze in Florida where since 1987 strange lights had been seen and photographed. Allegedly the lasers had indeed precipitated a number of sightings and it was presumably therefore hoped that the same success might be achieved amidst the crop fields.

I have to note that my enquiries in the USA, such as with abduction expert Dr Thomas Bullard plus inspection of some of the film taken at Gulf Breeze during 1992 thanks to optical physicist Dr Bruce Maccabee, leads me to conclude that some at least of the recent sightings in this town stem from locals who have become aware of the attention focused on them and have been sending up home-made hot air balloons and distress flares. The purpose is presumably to produce events to please the crowds that gather nightly by the bridge opposite the Pensacola naval base. I would not presume these account for everything witnessed in Gulf Breeze. These events are clearly a latter-day reaction to its pre-existent status as a famous UFO hot spot. However, they do have to be taken into account when assessing some of the floating orange balls of light reported in connection with some of Greer's experiments.

Whatever the truth, the researcher's laser light shows projected into the skies above Woodborough Hill near Alton Barnes were undoubtedly themselves the cause of several UFO sightings during late July. I received several calls about glowing patches of white light in the sky which I immediately explained from my personal sightings of similar projected beams despite not knowing that lasers were in use at the time.

Paul Fuller (*Crop Watcher*, July 1992) tells how he, Dr Ernie Peck (from Project Argus) and two leading American UFO investigators (Dennis Stacy from MUFON and Chris Talarski of CUFOS) all witnessed the lasers on the night of 21 July and how military helicopters, which frequent the area, as any regular visitor will attest, do seem to have gone to investigate these bright glowing ovals in the sky.

Many other misinterpretations of the laser lights followed. Indeed they were so powerful that reports of sightings were made to the police from up to thirty miles away. By 28 July I was receiving several phone calls a day channelled via BUFORA demanding to know why we were not responding to the conviction within large parts of the Wessex cereology movement that an epoch-making event was happening. Indeed one source accused BUFORA of covering up the event of the century that had occurred the day before. Since this event was also covered up by the entire world's media, none of whom mentioned it at all, BUFORA can hopefully be forgiven.

Colin Andrews later made public statements to the effect that his views on *South Today* had now been justified. The contact had happened. OVNI newsletter (October 1992) cites him as saying that it proved that 'some form of intelligence was at work' and that he and others witnessed 'a series of extraordinary events'.

A detailed account was finally offered by Chris Mansell in the *Circular* (October 1992). He told of the following sequence of events. He and a friend visited the Alton Barnes area to watch circles. On 23 July they had met up with Steven Greer and his colleagues from the team he called the Centre for the Study of Extraterrestrial Intelligence (CSETI). As a result Greer invited

Mansell and his friend to join their team in their efforts to establish contact with aliens and 'the agency concerned with the manufacture of crop circles'. Aside from using the powerful lights to beam codes and images, group meditation to mentally project such things was also part of the process.

On a very wet Saturday night, late on 26 July, they reached the Alton Priors area and owing to the weather moved to Woodborough Hill where a concrete road made passage easier. Participants in the several-day-old project decided to abandon their efforts for the night and some returned to their hotel but Mansell, his friend, Greer and another member of his CSETI team stayed on. It was still drizzling and they were just about to call it a night when Mansell saw a strip of rotating lights coloured orange, red, green and white. They all got out of the car and Greer 'immediately recognised it as what he called a "non-terrestrial craft" ... ' They watched it move around for about fifteen minutes until about 1.20 a.m. and Greer used his big lights to flash a message which the unseen dark object mirrored straight back at them via its own lights. This occurred several times, confirming the impression of intelligence. As they were watching the spectacle an army helicopter was heard in the distance, but not seen. To me, at least, this last news might suggest a military component to this affair. Perhaps some sort of exercise was underway with the response to the flashing lights thus becoming more simply understandable?

Colin Andrews seems to have been with a group of other people on a nearby hill who did not actually see the object but did see the field over which it had hovered briefly illuminated by a strong glow.

Sadly, no photographs of this event appear to have been taken as the cameras had been (according to one report) packed away due to the bad weather. But if this phenomenon was flying around for fifteen minutes and there was time to set up a searchlight and beam messages into the air surely someone ought to have been prepared to get visual proof of this anticipated event? If they did, no such evidence has yet been published.

By the next day the event was the buzz of the UFO world, hence the phone calls I received about our 'cover up' of the incident. This widespread awareness has to be judged against the fact that a single circle then appeared four days after the

UFO sighting not exactly at, but not far from, Woodborough Hill where the close encounter took place.

This was not the only extraordinary claim from summer 1992. The other stemmed from the aptly named UFO group, Contact UK, founded as the 'International Sky Scouts' years before by British peer Lord Clancarty (who wrote UFO books under his full name of Brinsley Le Poer Trench). Contact have been a moderate and rational data collection agency regarded with some respect in the UFO world. But in their magazine (*Awareness*, Vol 18 No 3) a quite amazing revelation was offered.

The editorial reported how this issue 'may be the most important in Contact International history'. Why? because one of their research team 'believes he is in telepathic contact with another life form'. And not just any life form. It turns out, according to an eight-page 'statement from Contact International' that follows, to be the one responsible for the creation of the crop circles.

The research team claims were long, complex and remarkably specific. Their contact had apparently lasted several months and even offered a self-portrait. The aliens described themselves as resembling a dentist's drill. Based on multiple-choice questions produced, I would guess, by something akin to automatic writing, a lot more 'data' emerged. For example, the entities come from the planet Metan and arrived on Earth on 20 March 1980. Some 950 of them fled a dying world to reach Earth and settled above two hundred sites of 'free Earth energy', the best of which were over England. Fifty-two 'Metans' live in the atmosphere above Britain and send 'parcels' of energy via the wind to their less well-off comrades moored above poorer parts of Earth. The Metans regard us as 'talented but foolish' and are producing the circles to establish harmony. They will only reveal their presence slowly (across a million years!) and do so by shooting energy pancakes at the ground, although these have to pass through a time warp first.

There is much more, but Contact's editors do (thankfully) realize that readers are 'not expected to believe all of this in one go'. However, the Metans have agreed to answer readers' questions ('Dear Abby' style) and these were solicited. Issues of *Awareness* in 1993 have already begun to carry this rather unique 'Agony Aunt' column and perhaps in a future edition of this book we will have more to say. For now it is enough just to imagine this fleet of marooned aliens sitting in their time warp thinking up new circles to bamboozle us with.

Conclusions

1992 was certainly an astonishing year for the crop circle world.

Circles did not entirely dry up in other parts of the world and Chris Rutkowski did some excellent work recording details of a few mostly simple marks found in the Canadian wheat belt.

In addition, there was some excellent follow-up by Andrew Collins of aboriginal legends in the Tully area of Queensland, Australia, continuing work I briefly did when I was in this rainforest region south of Cairns during September 1991. Strange lights have been reported for centuries and swirled circles have been regularly appearing in the matted reeds of the lagoons within banana and sugarcane plantations astride the Indian Ocean. They undoubtedly predate the arrival of Doug and Dave who, in fact, credit these marks with giving them the idea to fabricate circles back in England. Ironically the very day they broke their hoax story to the world I was in far north Queensland establishing that these January 1966 reed circles were indeed quite genuine and had been but an isolated example of a whole series of similar events found in that area.

The retrospective studies of the Tully area have been one of the most valuable ways that crop circle researchers have been able to bypass the hoaxing débâcles of recent summers. For cases such as this, far into the past, well outside of the pressures of Wessex and yet clearly 'real' circles in every sense of the word, must establish beyond much doubt that there is a genuine phenomenon still to be investigated.

The real circles have been swamped by human engineering and tainted by the excesses of critics, believers and the media alike. But when all of the hoaxers finally give up the ghost and the last journalist writes the final epitaph on the circle enigma there is now ample evidence to make a firm prediction that there will still be a few simple anomalies appearing in the crop fields – just as there always have been.

Earth Mysteries

This covers a multitude of areas revolving around the idea that the earth itself may possess forces and energies which, perhaps, in the distant past our ancestors might have been rather more in tune with than we are today thanks to our preference for a technological culture. This concept and other less exotic possibilities are adopted to try to understand why monuments such as the stone circles of southern England, the pyramids in Egypt or the lines scoured across the Nazca desert of South America do seem to have involved such immense effort presumably expended for some little-understood (but at the time quite profound) purpose.

There are both science-based aspects of earth mysteries, covering archaeology and historical research, and the rather more avant-garde fields that extend the research into regions that otherwise might be termed supernatural. We will look at progress during 1992 in both directions, but concentrate on those aspects that touch upon the paranormal. These will include some rather controversial areas, notably the existence or otherwise of the so-called Bermuda Triangle, which came to the fore during the year.

Historical earth mysteries

There are a number of conflicting theories about the origin of Britain's best-known ancient monument, the circle of standing stones at Stonehenge in Wiltshire. Probably the most popular is that it was created as a form of astronomical observatory, perhaps to participate in religious ceremonies or to measure the movement of sun and stars around the earth and so judge the seasons to aid in agriculture. In days long before calendars and watches this would have been a very useful device and similar purposes are often ascribed to other monuments the world over, although few have been reliably proven to be so linked.

A newcomer into the field in 1992 was meteorologist and physicist Dr Terence Meaden, better known for his plasma vortex theory regarding crop circles. Seemingly intrigued that crop circles have chosen to appear most often in and around the concentration of ancient sites in Wessex (notably Stonehenge and Avebury), he has looked for a historical explanation for why this might be so.

It is true that vast effort went into the creation of these monuments which have survived thousands of years of weathering to remain impressive even today. How much more magnificent they must have appeared when first created. The rock that the huge blocks of Stonehenge are made from is not local to Wiltshire. It was brought there from south Wales and that process itself must have been long and arduous. Indeed there have been (rather needless) speculations about aliens or levitation beams facilitating this work. But what the effort expended does show is that something really important to the ancient Britons who forged the monument must have lain behind its creation. Why not build an observatory where the stones originated to make life much simpler? There had to be a reason to move them many miles to Wiltshire.

Meaden has come up with the idea that the purpose might have been stimulated by the existence of crop circles in the fields of this area. If a rare phenomenon were occasionally gouging out these patterns it is quite likely it would be deified in some way by the local people of the time. He has extended his earlier speculations to develop a thesis whereby the vortex that he believes originates the circles was itself also part of the process.

He suggests that to the ancient mind a twisting corkscrew like a tornado coming out of the clouds and spiking the fertile earth so as to create a crop circle would produce the effect of bodily copulation. The earth has been looked upon as female in most religions, giving birth to nature as it does. Here the image of it being 'seeded' by a male force from above might well have been powerful.

Pursuing this idea, he has looked for patterns within monuments like Stonehenge and noticed how in midsummer (when the symbolism of the monument is most effective) the circular shadow cast by the main ring of stones appears to be 'penetrated' by the large upright 'heel stone'.

Meaden found other similar indications to extend his thesis but it has received a mixed response from the earth mysteries community. Even Paul Devereux, editor of the seminal journal the *Ley Hunter*, whilst cautiously welcoming some of the ideas, does think that he shows little awareness of, or at least offers little credit for, earlier work done on the interpretation of shadows at circle sites, notably Martin Brennan's research into such effects at ancient monuments in Ireland. None the less, it is a challenging new interpretation.

A fascinating illustration of how a quite different meteorological phenomenon has also been adapted to such neolithic sites is the work reported by Donald Cyr, also a crop circle enthusiast and leader in the 'Stonehenge Viewpoint' movement of the USA. He shows an intriguing relationship between ice crystal halos and the geometry found within locations such as Stonehenge.

Ice crystal halos are reflected images in the sky formed by sunlight bouncing off crystals in the higher atmosphere. The most common type is refered to as a 'sun dog' and leaves a white circle of light in the sky at its most concentrated point. These have occasionally been interpreted as UFOs by eyewitnesses even in quite recent times. There is nothing fantastic in the possibility that such phenomena when seen in the ancient past might have been interpreted religiously. Indeed rare forms of halo produce a near crucifix shape which, of course, has had a whole new meaning stamped upon it over the past two millenia.

Thousands of years ago the northern latitudes of earth were still slowly recovering from the last incursions of the ice age and temperatures were generally colder than at present. Ice crystals would have been more prevalent in the atmosphere and halos probably seen more frequently. It is quite possible to imagine how sites where they were commonly observed might have been revered in some way.

But is there any actual evidence for this fanciful theory? Cyr thinks there is. He reports on computer experiments to try to test out what he admits began as a visionary experience of a starburst of ice crystal halos above stone circles. Cyr had calculated the positions where mock suns could theoretically form at sunrise and plotted lines from the centre of a circle to all of these against an overhead plan of Stonehenge. It matched quite well, showing stones at the ice halo points.

However, he reports a lot of difficulty persuading others to take his ideas seriously. Only during 1992 did he convince a computer scientist, Joe Boucher, at General Research Corporation in Santa Barbara, California, to create a program that could be tested against other megalithic monuments.

Perhaps the greatest hope was afforded by Avebury in Wiltshire, a giant circle of stones almost bisecting the village, and the second most famous in Britain. However, whilst some indications were found that on certain days of the year some of the stones exactly matched points where mock suns could occur, the most common position (22 degrees either side of the sun's actual location) was never favoured and the evidence proved rather weaker than anticipated. Other locations proved more successful, notably a small circle near Aviemore in Scotland. Donald Cyr now wonders if this computer program might not be a useful way of determining which megalithic sites have some sort of astronomical basis and which do not.

The importance of sites such as Aviemore in Scotland also illustrates a common misunderstanding about earth mystery sites. They are not only found in England, but appear in many unexpected locations. For example, Larry Meylak reported in *Stonehenge Viewpoint* on the carbon dating of megaliths uncovered on the Mediterranean island of Malta which show that they stem from around 3200 BC. They have very similar features to British sites, including stones that appear to act as a window to the sun at the summer solstice, one of the main indicators of their astronomical significance and a key reason why each midsummer the Wessex area sees a regular invasion of modern Druids and other New Age communities.

Other locations peppered with impressive sites include Celtic-influenced nations such as France (especially Carnac to the west) and Ireland (one of the best being at Newgrange) plus some rather more surprising regions such as Sweden, which boasts megalithic circles and standing stones very similar to Britain's.

However, not all historical earth mystery research is concerned with ancient sites like these. The subject also takes in some more unusual byways.

Andy Roberts lectured to the earth mysteries beanfeast (the

annual 'Ley Hunter moot') on the significance of the area within which the September 1992 event was held – Hebden Bridge in the Calderdale valley of West Yorkshire. This region has been settled for several thousand years and has legends aplenty, as reported in his writings, including a 1992 book about the ghosts and legends of the area. It is particularly noteworthy for a plethora of carved stone heads about the size of a fist. Some slightly larger ones are found on the gable ends of houses (at Greetland for instance) and on the crowns of bridges (as at Hebden Bridge itself). They appear to be there to ward off spirits and to serve as guardians.

An amusing story told by Andy concerned the stone head dug up at Rishworth Hall near Keighley. The family who found it kept it in their garage and claim they were plagued by ill luck, as is said to befall anyone who disturbs one of these millstone grit creations. They saw phantoms, lost money and went through a gruelling time. So they decided to sell it. Andy Roberts and co-researcher David Clarke put in a bid at the auction and won the prize. Since possessing it they have had no bad luck, indeed if anything better luck than before, Andy mused! Then the former owner of the land on which it was unearthed came forward to report that he made it himself in the early 1970s and buried it 'to confuse archaeologists of the future'. This anecdote might well suggest that luck is a state of mind rather more than something more absolute.

Another quite different aspect of earth mystery research is the attempt to unravel the truth about legends. One of the most famous is that of King Arthur and his knights. Did such a person ever exist or is he merely a myth? Many places lay claim to be the original Camelot but none has ever been established to total satisfaction.

In mid 1992 researcher Ron Fletcher created quite a stir in the Gloucestershire area when a possible new origin for the king was uncovered, effectively challenging what had been until then the favoured location, Glastonbury in Somerset. Fletcher, along with Danny Sullivan, published a more detailed account of their work in *Gloucestershire Earth Mysteries*, 14. The basis of this latest relocation of Arthur is a translation of some poems from *Four Ancient Books of Wales*. According to the researchers this clearly states that the main events took place around Woodchester near Stroud in the Cotswolds.

Rather wonderful juggling of words, translations, possible meanings of both and then a charting of the way in which place names have adapted over more than a thousand years of history are the basis for the wide disagreement on who may be correct. Fletcher makes a case for the misinterpretation of words like Silcestrie in the original that to some indicate Silbury but to Fletcher Siver Street between Woodchester and Chalford.

No doubt such jigsaw puzzle solving from scattered bits of evidence for what to many is an unproven historical event will continue to go on, but it is another aspect of this fascinating field of earth mystery research.

The Nazca lines

The mystery of the lines on the Nazca plain of Peru is one that continues to captivate researchers in the sub-field called geomancy. This looks at geographical anomalies and tries to chart their meaning and purpose.

The intrigue of the lines etched into the desert floor on these heatseared plains is that they are only really visible in their true splendour from the air. From the ground they are a pale shadow of their glorious selves. They depict animals and also have long straight tracks that traverse miles of terrain in precisely laid out geometric formations. Yet they are very old – up to 1400 years for some of the features. Certainly they must have been created at a time when there was no aerial capability for the local people. So how were they done?

Their most famous student was Maria Reiche who spent years living in the area, devoting her days to an attempt to figure out the meaning of this magnificent spectacle. She was able to show how they followed a geometric framework of design that must have been worked out in advance.

Nobody knows why the lines were created; perhaps for ceremonial or religious purposes. Scholars of the 'ancient astronaut' school of thought have often suggested that aliens in spaceships must have guided the natives to produce them. On the other hand there have been brave attempts to show that, using only indigenous facilities and the knowledge of the day, tethered hot air balloons might have been produced and the architects of the designs might have overflown the terrain to guide the workers. Possibly these patterns were meant to be a tribute to sky gods.

David Browne is an archaeologist with the Royal Commission on Ancient and Historical Monuments and he reported to the 1992 Ley Hunter moot on his latest field work in Peru. He had not originally gone there to look at the lines, but once there you cannot miss their beauty, he reported. They had only been known since the arrival of modern air travel and were at first thought to be very old canals. Relatively little work has been done in this remote area to try to unravel their true essence, but they do have interesting parallels with the 'ley' system of straight lines said by earth mystery students to have been traced linking stone circle monuments in northern Europe. Even Reiche, sadly, published very little about her findings, so Browne's research is more than welcome.

The pampas on which the lines appear is a bleak terrain subject to sudden flooding and inhabited by dangerous animals and few people. The underlying rock is darker than the weathered surface and so it is relatively easy to excavate this and produce the visible lines. Browne argues that the intense labour often speculated about to create them is overemphasized. As a surveyor he has calculated that 10,000 people working for about ten years could have produced all the known lines. Equally he challenges the conclusion about their need to be appreciated from the air. Some can be seen from hills, and given the amount of weathering over hundreds of years they might originally have been clearer and so more readily visible from sea level.

He notes three main types of form: 'biomorphs' (human and animal shapes), lines and geometric symbols and vast cleared areas. They seem to date from different eras over hundreds of years from before 600 AD onward. Some even overlie older shapes like chalk on a used blackboard.

One of his most important findings is that the attempt to impose a Stonehenge-like astronomical interpretation on the lines fails. The animal shapes do not reflect star constellations. The ancient Incas had a very different sky to look at and could not have applied the same kind of logic as Europeans did. The feel of the lines is very much Andean culture, not European.

Browne suggests that most of the lines have no clear astronomical significance. So there have been other attempts to understand them, for example as a kind of map of human and religious structures within the Nazca society. To some extent the lines resemble footpaths leading to cleared areas of trapezoids which might be viewed as huge assembly points. However, other lines wind around in big spirals to reach their destination and would have taken a very long time to walk.

The mysteries of the Nazca lines have certainly yet to be resolved but they clearly represent one of the most intriguing challenges and the most wonderful visual anomalies on the earth's surface. Given today's better communications it is possible that they will receive greater attention in the future and more progress will be made.

Earth energies

In Strange Phenomena Investigations' *Enigmas* magazine (May 1992) Scottish earth mystery researcher Ron Halliday reported on his research into Arthur's Seat in Edinburgh. This hill has many long associations with folklore which suggests that it was the doorway to another world or dimension. In recent times lights in the sky have been seen nearby.

Halliday has traced energy pathways, akin to leys, which seem to intersect in this area. He likens them to a form of electrical power and speculates that standing stones and other monuments may have been placed there to amplify this hidden energy bursting forth from the earth itself and so ensure that it responded by granting fertility and other natural favours.

This concept of an 'earth energy' is much to the fore of earth mysteries research and many attempts have been made to tap into it at key sites and understand its nature. Many of the zones where this energy is said to focus occur around the earth. In *Earthquest* (Winter 1992) Andy Collins reports on his research into the Chic-ah-bunnah, strange lights seen for millenia by the Aborigine inhabitants around Cairns in Queensland. They associate them with spirits in the dreamtime but they are really floating, drifting balls of energy akin to those seen all over the earth. Collins' co-researcher Claire Noble tells of how the Australian Chic-ah-bunnah around Mount Tyson near Tully (home of modern-day crop circles by the dozen) takes the form of a 'strange blue light' which is 'frightful to behold' and how it is seen by locals 'rushing through the air'. It only grounds itself at certain sacred sites, according to Aboriginal tradition, which is exactly like similar legends from all over the world associated with these lights, energies and earth mystery sites.

There is clearly a common denominator behind these energies, or telluric forces. Earth mystery kingpin Paul Devereux has given them the name 'earthlight' and believes that they are a product of forces from within the earth but are also interactive with human consciousness in as yet little-understood ways.

One of the best locations for regularly seeing what locals often term 'spooklights' is the Marfa region of Texas. Here glowing orange lights are frequently reported at night drifting along the mountains, and a sign on the local highway even points them out. They have been captured on film many times, often enough to establish their reality beyond any reasonable doubt.

In *Ley Hunter* 117 Edson Hendricks reports on thirty-three pictures he took at this position which were studied by John Derr of the US geological survey. Derr presented these at a conference at Princeton in April 1992. The importance of these new photographs is that they were taken in relatively daytime-like conditions which allows sight of the landscape. This eliminates often-presented theories about car headlights on distant roads being refracted like a mirage.

Derr has made extensive investigations of such balls of light seen in association with earthquake activity the world over. In April 1992 he announced the discovery of a link between the injection and extraction of fluids into the earth's crust and localized outbreaks of earthlights.

It does seem that both grand-scale tectonic stress underneath the earth's surface, as in the slippage of major fault lines, and more small-scale, even human-made, activities such as mining work and the filling and emptying of reservoirs, can all lead to outbreaks of earthlight activity in these areas. This has been claimed by earth mystery and some UFO researchers for ten years, but now we have important professional support for the theory. It also has the backing of Dr Michael Persinger, from Laurentian University in Canada, who did a computer plot of thousands of light phenomena and found similar correlations with fault lines, mining and reservoirs.

What might seem like a minor academic matter could potentially have dramatic repercussions. For it may ultimately prove possible to understand why some areas 'leak' energy as earthlights on a regular basis, as at Marfa in Texas and what appear to be identical 'window areas' around fault zones such as Hessdalen in Norway and Todmorden/Bacup in the Pennine Hills of England. These have also produced so many sightings and photographs of an identical nature that their status cannot be disputed.

Other areas, such as the San Andreas Fault zone of California, do not work in the same way and instead unleash their energy in sudden, infrequent and highly destructive bursts that generate massive earthquakes. If a method could be found to turn a destructive quake zone into a steady bleeder of energy as earthlights, lives might be saved and tourist attractions created from the displays of light in the sky. This would be one of the most valuable contributions ever made by a subject that most scientists consider either supernatural or nonsensical.

The Gaia hypothesis

To some earth mystery researchers the earth is not merely traversed by these lines of energy; it is actually a living entity. They call it 'Gaia' (the earth spirit) and believe that much that is wrong with today's society is a result of our treatment of the earth and its reaction to what we are doing.

If you kick an elephant it might kick you back. If the earth is alive then it might in its own way be wreaking its revenge on homo sapiens for our raping and pillaging of its precious resources. This is the emotive terminology that many New Age practitioners of the Gaia hypothesis use and which in recent years has made saints and sinners (depending on your viewpoint) of writers such as former TV sports presenter David Icke. During August 1992 Icke was, in fact, star guest at the major crop circle jamboree, illustrating the way in which these divergent ideas have become intertwined within that rapidly mutating phenomenon. However, in the *Journal of Meteorology* (October 1992) Mark Sunlin from Saratoga, California, asks whether the whole Gaia concept might not be misunderstood by its adherents and detractors alike.

It began as a climatology theory devised by James Lovelock in the 1970s. He saw the earth's weather systems as a self-regulating affair rather like a thermostat, which turns the heat up automatically if a building gets too cold, or down again if it gets too warm. It has achieved increased attention, Sunlin says, because of the new awareness of the dangers of the greenhouse effect, global warming and other forms of response by the atmosphere and biosphere of earth to things that we have done in modern times, notably the gaping holes in the ozone layer.

Sunlin notes that Lovelock never intended his 'earth as a living cell' idea to be more than allegory, not the literal interpretation seized upon by the supernaturalists. To some, anything that goes wrong is a tantrum by mother earth; for example crop circles are planetary 'zits'!

Sunlin's paper, which makes telling points and was vetted at the manuscript stage by Lovelock himself, may warn of the danger of over-elaboration of the theory. Already computer expert Dr Jacques Vallee has, seemingly quite independently, come up with what he calls the 'control' theory for UFO events which also likens their interaction with human consciousness to a thermostat, regulating belief systems by modifying the way the product appears to the eyewitness. There are clear signs that the new esoteric wing of the cereology community want to impose this kind of solution on the metamorphosis displayed by the crop circles (which, as we saw in the last chapter, is mostly illusionary in truth, because these complex designs are probably hoaxes.)

There is even a degree of evidence within parapsychology for this kind of Gaia-based approach to paranormal phenomena such as telepathy and precognition. Rupert Sheldrake's morphogenetic fields theory (which, as you again saw, is also gaining a toehold in the crop circle world) is another fascinating idea that shares more than a little with Gaia but is equally independent of it.

Whilst it may be true that the simultaneous appearance over the past decade of closely parallel ideas to explain subjects as diverse as climatology, UFOs, crop circles and parapsychology could point towards some kind of fundamental truth being sensed, it is also wise to recall Sunlin's cautions. However, it is also sensible not to discard the new directions that the Gaia style of approach has introduced. Paul Devereux has been a figure within the earth mysteries field who has led others into fruitful territory by looking beyond the obvious.

Never is that more true than in trends which arose during 1992, taking the field towards a closer understanding of the role that consciousness might play within earth mysteries. Devereux himself published two important books in this direction and *Ley Hunter* was full of significant pieces reflecting the trend.

In *Ley Hunter* 116 a close look was taken at shamanism. Shamans have existed in many tribal cultures – including the North American Indians, the Aborigines and the African nations. Societies we refer to as primitive consider the 'medicine man' to be a focal point, acting as a conduit to inner realities via what are easily recognisable as altered states of consciousness. Although we tend to be dismissive, there is strong evidence for the significance of some of the recorded experiences. Also it appears that our western technological culture cannot exist without our own shamans. Because that, to all intents and purposes, is exactly what mediums or UFO contactees are. The very fact that we afford such people the attention and reverence that we do may well indicate that subconsciously we know that they plug a vital gap in our culture.

Devereux referred to the new directions of 1992 as a 'paradigm shift' and explained how he has come to realize that the 'energy lines' concept for leys or pathways between ancient sites (from Nazca to Arthur's Seat) is 'humbug'. He announced that for years people had been playing with theories about 'lines of power' but that now 'playtime was over!'

So what does he propose to replace this concept with? He looks at shamanistic rituals the world over and the importance of 'straight lines' or 'threads' to form a bridge to the soul. Indeed, we even see this in modern mediumistic practices. The 'silver cord' said by Spiritualists to link the spirit body to the material world in out-of-body states has much in common with Devereux's ideas.

Focusing on some discoveries from Germany and Holland of very old, very straight tracks leading to burial sites, Devereux ponders the significance of a common phrase in the English language, 'dead straight'. Why 'dead', he asks? He begins to suspect that the lines across our planet may have been mapped out by shamans as what he calls 'spirit ways'. He proposes that research focus on the potential discovery of these long-lost 'dead straight' spirit paths, which may well have physical manifestations on the landscape. Some early findings have been published in *Ley Hunter* 117 and a new exploration is under way.

Parallel to this, research is also progressing to find a link between human consciousness and these ancient sites of so-called earth energy, which Devereux (from his earthlights concept) clearly believes in as an actual reality, rather than simply as a state of mind.

For some time what is called the Dragon Project has been using scientific monitoring equipment to try to tap into any hidden energy sources such as might exist at standing stones. But more recently they have expanded into new territory, effectively duplicating the Aborigine dreamtime. In fact, people are sleeping at, or within, key ancient sites where these energy foci are suspected and their experiences, notably their dreams, are being recorded. The project is called 'Operation Interface'.

One of their earliest findings was that sites which they recorded as having certain ores or as generating radon, a mildly radioactive gas from under the earth, triggered altered states of consciousness more often. A three-year experiment is now under way with ten 'dreamers' sleeping semi-regularly at four selected ancient sites. Dr Stanley Krippner, a San Francisco psychologist and specialist in dream states, will be monitoring the tape-recorded output of the resultant dreams. Paul and Charla Devereux, overseeing the project, naturally do not reveal any outcome until it is over because this might compromise the data, but they are getting consistent imagery which might suggest a 'tuning in' to something sensed about the site in question.

This is a fascinating idea which they would like to pursue in other countries and they are seeking volunteers. Seriously committed people prepared to suffer the minor hardships involved should write to the *Ley Hunter* address (see page 188).

Window areas

In the world of strange phenomena we soon learn that not all ideas that look good, are good, and not everything that we would like to be true, is true.

One of the most alluring concepts has been that of 'window areas', focal points for strange phenomena, or, to some, doorways to another reality. In its basic sense these do exist. More than enough material has been gathered from fields such as earth mysteries, UFOlogy etc. to show that some locations have far more than their fair share of mysterious happenings. My 1992 book *UFOs and How to See Them* (Anaya) gives a pictorial guide to the fifty major sites around the world.

Research in the earth mysteries field has also uncovered reasons why this might be true, finding linking patterns involving geophysical processes in the rocks beneath these areas themselves.

However, this (literally!) down-to-earth concept has been tarnished by the sensationalist approach, hyping bestsellers by turning something into a 'deadly triangle' or 'zone of fear'. Indeed, the impact of this is shown by the fact that in 1983 when I wrote my book *The Pennine UFO Mystery* which charts the history of events in one hillside window area, the publishers understandably wanted to cash in by calling it 'The Pennine Triangle'. Although the area *is* (unusually for once) in this case a real geographical triangle I declined to agree because the term is badly compromised.

It has been damaged, of course, by the much touted existence of the 'Bermuda Triangle', possibly one of the most misrepresented phenomena of recent times. For a start it never really was a triangle, just a huge expanse of Atlantic Ocean somewhere between the east coast of the USA, Bermuda and the Azores. Its size and shape fluctuated wildly from authority to authority and, being one of the most heavily shipped routes and busiest air corridors there is, it was hardly surprising that it had more than the average number of disappearances and accidents.

However, once the idea took hold that there was something inexplicable about these incidents, the concept developed a life of its own, spawning imitators as in the oceans around Japan or the Bass Strait of Tasmania, and what began as an idea with some merit quickly turned into a mystery that was all hype and little substance.

For some years, paranormal researchers have accepted that many of the famed disappearances of ships and aircraft are not quite so sinister as they seem. Often key facts make all the difference, once you discover them. If you are told that a huge tanker sailing across the Atlantic vanishes in calm weather and no trace of it is ever found then this sounds very strange indeed. If you then learn that it was carrying a highly volatile or explosive cargo, that there were unconfirmed reports of a huge explosion being heard and that the sea at this point is so deep that no wreckage would ever be visible, it becomes rather less of a mystery and just a tragedy.

Of course, there were some rather less well explained incidents, but these also occur all over the world. The evidence that they occur any more often in the so called Bermuda Triangle (particularly in relation to the amount of traffic that passes through this region) is by no means as clear cut as you might think.

During 1992 the subject came to the fore again for three reasons. In 1991 it had been announced that 'Flight 19' had been found. This is one of the real gems of the Triangle mystery and if, as many media sources announced, it had now been resolved, this would have effectively dismantled the last remaining foundation for the phenomenon. However, in 1992 the truth, which was not so well reported, emerged, and this changed things somewhat.

Flight 19 was a training mission of five US Navy aircraft which left Florida in December 1945 on a routine flight in fine weather. They never returned. All sorts of speculations about what might have happened have been offered, ranging from entry into another dimension to kidnap by aliens. Indeed in his 1978 movie *Close Encounters of the Third Kind* Steven Spielberg builds the story into the plot with the aliens returning the Flight 19 crew decades later mysteriously unaged!

The sceptical view of the disappearance is quite a sensible one. It argues that they simply made a wrong turning and, being inexperienced pilots, may easily have become disorientated over the Florida Keys. These are strips of islands that all look very much alike. If the young fliers thought from landmarks that they were heading inland but were instead travelling in almost any other direction, they could have gone for hours without seeing anything but sea, until they realised their error too late and ran out of fuel.

This had been no more than a theory for many years, but it received a massive boost with the alleged discovery in shallow water of what was said to be near perfect remains of Flight 19. The end of the mystery was pronounced, but when later exploration was able to look more closely at the wreckage it was discovered that these were similar aircraft but not Flight 19. That mission remains as lost as ever.

However, a new scientific theory was proposed in 1992 to try to account for the assorted vanishings. American geochemist Dr Richard McIver came up with the idea that deadly gas bombs might be to blame.

It is true that the exceptionally explosive methane gas is trapped in chemicals on the sea bed inside the Triangle area. McIver suggests that it might escape in giant bubbles rushing to the surface. The resulting explosion could tear a ship to pieces and scatter its debris for miles. Or if the bubble flew skywards it might similarly destroy an aircraft. He also thinks the methane bubble theory might account for other anomalies sometimes reported by sailors and aviators in the region, such as strange clouds and magnetic fields.

Interesting as this novel idea may be, it seems to stretch credulity somewhat. How common would such bubbles have to be to now and again wipe out ships and planes with direct hits? And if they are as common as that why are bubbles not being seen far more often without causing impacts?

In May 1992 I was fortunate enough to hear aviator Martin Caidin describe his own first-hand experiences in the Triangle whilst we attended the Fortean Research Conference at Lincoln, Nebraska. Caidin is a world famous flier whose missions have often caused headlines. He is also a born storyteller and his accounts of cyborgs and space flights have inspired television series like *The Six Million Dollar Man* and Hollywood movies. His experiences are colourful and entertaining. For instance, he told of a flight on an Air Force plane from the American coast to Bermuda and then on to the Azores in 1960. Radar called to advise they were 1 hour 20 minutes from landing on Bermuda yet, mystifyingly, there was the island in front of them for all to see. As they flew on it became clear that, impossible though it might seem, they were getting no closer, so they climbed and descended to try to figure out this riddle. Nothing worked. They stayed as far away from the island as ever. Finally, everything returned to normal and they began to approach. Upon reaching Bermuda they were an hour late and the fuel consumption showed that they had used 2 hours 20 minutes worth of fuel to fly what the radar had indicated to be the normal distance.

Anomalies of space and time are more interesting within the Bermuda Triangle than many of the convoluted disappearance stories. Caidin claims an experience like this in 1986 when he was flying with several experienced pilots on a Catalina sea plane bound for demonstration flights in England. Over sea east of Bermuda all the compasses suddenly spun wildly as if swamped by a magnetic field. The equipment on board was state-of-the-art (it was even capable of detecting faxes directed from satellites to give pictures of the sky and chart one's course.) But nothing was working. In addition, they were within what Caidin called a 'lemon meringue sky' with nothing visible, not even the aircraft wing tips. They climbed to 8000 feet and down to 200 feet but there was no alteration in the conditions. So they simply headed towards the lightest patch of sky and after four hours broke free into clear blue normality. With that the radio and all other equipment functioned properly again. He claims there is some kind of strange field over this part of the earth's surface and alleges that even NASA has suffered mystery power blackouts when spacecraft such as Skylab have orbited overhead.

Certainly, there do appear to be more than enough stories such as this to suggest something odd is going on. I got a report first-hand from a sailor on a tanker who says that for some minutes he found himself wandering around a 'ghost ship', with all his fellow crew having disappeared. There was no sound and the sea and sky blended into a uniform steel-grey canopy, seemingly akin to Martin Caidin's 'lemon meringue' effect. Eventually, the sailor rounded a bulkhead and there were his colleagues desperately seeking him and asking why he had not been anywhere on the ship. With this discovery the sky and sea had returned to full colour normality and all the sounds that had vanished returned.

Perhaps, after all, there is more to the Bermuda Triangle than meets the eye.

Extra-terrestrials

In many respects 1992 was the year of the aliens. With clever foresight NASA had seized upon the fact that it was the five hundredth anniversary of the epic voyage by Columbus to discover the 'new world'. Capturing the spirit of the pioneer explorer they launched the most ambitious ever search for worlds beyond the earth. Scientists were in effect planned to tune in to ET.

The idea that we are not alone in the cosmos is a dream that dates back centuries. It is the basis of much of science fiction and yet we still do not know if it is myth or reality.

We have learnt a great deal over recent years about the history and vastness of the universe. Billions of suns like our own stretch out for endless light years and, if our theories of stellar evolution are valid, some, probably many of them, are sufficiently similar to have produced solar systems not unlike our neighbouring planets. Beyond that point it is a game of statistics. If only a small fraction of stars have planets, if only a very few of these are like earth, if only on rare occasions do these have conditions likely to evolve into life, then however cautiously you do the mathematics you still end up with a myriad inhabited worlds. This is simply because a minute fraction of an unbelievably huge number still works out to be rather a lot.

However, this in itself brings problems. If there are many life-forms out there as proclaimed by imaginative television series such as *Star Trek*, then why are none of them visiting the earth probing our lifestyles or swapping trade secrets? Some planets would have to be more advanced than we, because our sun is very much a middle-of-the-road affair of no great antiquity or youth. As such there must be races far ahead of our capabilities and quite able to tour the universe. It only takes one of these to have 'done the rounds' or perhaps colonized the galaxy for us to have evidence for their existence, but we do not. This classic dilemma is known as the Fermi paradox.

Nevertheless, we are still desperate not to be alone, so we keep on searching. The methods we can use are limited by our own technology. A hundred years ago it was suggested we create a giant mirror and flash morse code signals at Mars. Today, our new toy is communication via electromagnetic radiation (i.e. radio or television) so we twiddle our dials on radio telescopes and hope to intercept a message from somewhere.

This process is immensely complex. Not only are there trillions of stars to point at but there are countless frequencies to tune into. If you do not have your dial on exactly the right station at the precise time when a programme is transmitted you will miss it even if you are lucky and chance to point the aerial at the right part of the sky.

Previous efforts since the birth of radio astronomy forty years ago have been limited by this needle in a haystack frustration. The basis of the Project Columbus programme which began in October 1992 is vastly improved computer technology which allows thousands of frequencies to be scanned at once. In this way it will still take years to sample all the options, covering the thousand most likely stars within a hundred light years of earth. But at least this becomes a possibility not a hopeless task.

Telescopes in California, Puerto Rico and Australia will scour the skies for ten years, if necessary, to seek out that elusive intelligent signal from the background hiss of space. Some hundred million dollars is being expended.

The *Financial Times* reviewed this matter on 10 October and took great pains to point out that SETI (the search for extraterrestrial intelligence) should 'not be confused with the fringe activities of UFO hunters'. This may be so, but I know, having talked with them, that at least two scientists in the US and Australia working on the NASA project do not consider UFOlogy a waste of space. They appreciate that for the relatively trivial sums involved in keeping tabs on progress the potential benefits for SETI, however small they may eventually prove to be, are ignored at the peril of science.

However, the real trouble with all of this fevered searching is that our wonderful 'new' technology is useless in terms of interstellar contact. To send a radio message to the very nearest star and then get an immediate reply will take nearly nine years.

So even if some aliens on Proxima Centauri tune into Columbus we will not know that until 2001!

In fact, this represents the ideal situation. The stars which are the more likely candidates involve return contact times of decades or centuries – something of a conversation stopper. At present we have nothing better available to use, so we do what we can, of course. But it is wise to be realistic and appreciate that it is pretty unlikely that any aliens will be chatting to us via this feeble technology. More likely they will have a better, faster method that we cannot yet imagine and might not discover until centuries from now. At which point we, like these aliens, will regard this hundred-million-dollar escapade as the quaint but unworkable gimmickry of the twentieth century mind, a bit like Jules Verne's technologically serious, but utterly impractical, method of reaching the moon by building a giant shotgun.

In any case, having seen the scientific protocol explaining what to do in the event of a message, I doubt we will learn the news as quickly as you might hope. They would have to duplicate the message, disassemble the computer equipment, rebuild it, replace it, and then, no doubt, ask the US president to time his speech to fit in with the peak television news and the current economic situation. This caution is necessary to prevent mistaking a natural radiating stellar source for an intelligent signal, but it means that you and I will be amongst the last to know.

Are they already here?

This question has a surprising number of people, especially in the USA, who seem ready to answer in the affirmative.

There are numerous claims of alien contact, with entities interacting directly with humans. These have been on the increase in recent years (see my book *Aliens: The real story* Hale, 1993, for a full discussion.) During 1992 many people had things to say about the matter, illustrating the breadth of opinion that it attracts.

Ironically, I created a minor flap when I lectured at a specially convened conference titled 'ET or not ET?' held at UMIST (University of Manchester Institute of Science and Technology). Some words from my paper were widely circulated in national and regional news sources, but were a tad misleading taken out of the context of my full presentation.

The *Birmingham Evening Mail* (25 April) had the headline 'UFO hidden invasion warning', noting that I said that 'people who believed they had sighted ... creatures from outer space could instead be having their minds probed from afar ... The phenomenon is vastly more widespread than people believe. It is as if aliens ... have found a different way to select certain people to make contact with in this more subtle way. We have a kind of hidden invasion which we know relatively little about.'

Events later in 1992 were to support my words, but what I was stressing was that claims of alien contact have a fundamental problem. They are clearly routed through the consciousness of human beings, appearing in a visionary form and disappointingly lacking in tangible physical evidence. However, they are too consistent to be mere hallucinations, because they have none of the imaginative breadth of science fiction books, television series and movies. They appear to reflect a reality that is more or less the same the world over but is much more 'real' within inner space than it is in the realms of outer reality.

If speed-of-light contact by radio is too slow, it may be that advanced aliens will use methods adapted from an understanding of consciousness. Modern physics suggests that this is the essence of physical reality anyhow and there are some grounds for considering it a timeless, spaceless field of energy not necessarily constrained by the same time limitations that radio must be. We may legitimately surmise that contact on a direct consciousness-to-consciousness basis, if at all possible, would be a superior method of interstellar liaison. All I am really noting is that the internal evidence within alien contact claims actually supports this 'mind communication' concept better than it does a fleet of intersteller 'Captain Kirks' roaming the universe in souped-up space shuttles.

In *UFO Brigantia* (Summer 1992) a fascinating interview between Andy Roberts and Eddie Bullard emphasized this point. Bullard, a folklore researcher from the University of Indiana, made it clear why he took a deep interest in this modern plague of 'alien contact' stories which have flooded the world during the past twenty years. 'I was hoping I would be able to scotch the whole thing,' Bullard reports uncompromisingly. As it turned out that was not to prove possible. Instead he found impressive patterns in what was by far the biggest and best academic study of over 700 detailed investigation reports ... 'There was a great deal of consistency of repetition. Much more so than what I have found in other folk narratives where there is a lot more variation ... I cannot say these things are folk narratives in the same sense as any other folk narratives, because they are not behaving like [them]...'

Of particular note is the way that the claim has an order and pattern so precise it can almost be predicted in advance. People of both sexes, usually in their early adulthood, of above average intelligence and (according to several independent psychological studies) without evidence of psychopathology, are claiming sudden interaction with strange entities who exhibit power and control over them, usually take them to an unknown room and often perform some medical tests on them, which not infrequently involve taking ova and sperm samples (or suggestions that they are so doing). Information is usually then imparted and the victim is returned to his/her own environment with memory not uncommonly all but blocked and yet with deep phobia and trauma which has been measured to be similar to that suffered by women who have been raped. Commonly there is little, if any, physical evidence that the event really occurred, but an undoubted response to it as if it had. Parallels and patterns that emerge from various cultures (with some differences but usually of detail rather than overall theme) argue counter to the lack of hard evidence and suggest that some real contact occurred.

Bullard ably defended charges that only one or two researchers world-renowned for probing these cases (New York artist Budd Hopkins being the best known) have produced this database, thus biasing the sample. He points out that in his research 'of 103 of the really good cases [i.e. with most follow up data] there were something like fifty different investigators ... that's a lot of hands in the stew to come out with a fair amount of consistency ... ' Overall he is forced into a difficult state of indecision. He says 'There are times when I look at them and I think these things must be psychological, there's just no way these things can be real. Other times I look at it and I don't see how they can be anything but...'

Serious researchers of these perplexing cases face up to this sort of dilemma rather than hide from it. This has provoked some extremes of attitude.

Timothy Good, a British classical musician, publicly well known because his views on the subject strike a chord in many people, takes the line in his books (such as his *Alien Liaison*, Arrow 1992) that 'contact has been established'. He is clear that this is physical contact and told the *Hastings Observer* (23 October) that 'I think some of them are extremely dangerous ... that's another reason why the Government are reluctant to make statements about this subject.' Indeed, he presents stories and rumours (not universally accepted even by the UFO community) that alien craft have crashed and bodies may even have been recovered, that in the Nevada desert a place called 'Dreamland' houses alien craft which the US military have actually flown. Like many, he suspects a major global conspiracy of silence.

Whilst I admire Tim's fortitude and respect his views I personally have to say I interpret this evidence quite differently and struggle to understand how any government that could not hide a burglary in the Watergate building could keep secret nearly fifty years of research into crashed spaceships, captured alien bodies and secret flights of wondrous technology. Would not some deathbed confessions or leaks of hard evidence have emerged by now? Just one photo of a grounded spaceship or pickled alien would do more than a dozen third-hand rumours.

None the less, this conviction is strong within society (displaying what has been aptly called the 'cry of a lonely species') and Tim Good's book sales and lecture audiences worldwide prove that there are more people willing to believe what he preaches than want to hear middle-of-the-road or sceptical assessments. We do *not* want to be alone.

Others take the line even further. Geoff Freed, as reported by the *Grimsby Telegraph* (3 November) is said to believe that 'aliens arrived here soon after we swung down from the trees', that 'religion is man made' and that a vast game of disinformation and preparation is under way, seeding the truth slowly to the world at large. When the grand announcement is made about alien presence on earth it will not come as quite such a culture shock.

I have had claims like this made to me by top-level sources, but the trouble I come up against is that if you believe that both information and disinformation are being spread about the subject (as I do) then how do you know which is which at any particular time?

David Jacobs, professor of history at Temple University in the USA, is a man who has certainly put his credibility on the line over these cases. Twenty years ago he made a major contribution by writing an unrivalled thesis on the historical debate between science, government and alien contact believers. Whilst working on its sequel he became sidetracked by the new wave of claims that human beings were being abducted by aliens and has spent recent years probing sixty cases first hand. The extraordinary patterns he claims to have unearthed were first published in 1992 in his book *Secret Life* (Simon and Schuster).

In August he visited Britain and I was pleased to lecture with him at a special event organized at Manchester University. Although our approaches to the question are very different, nobody knows the correct interpretation and at this stage it is vital to retain an open mind.

Jacobs' minute assessment of the medical procedures reported by victims of alien kidnap has telling points. For example, he notes that 'we do not have a single example of the beings listening to anybody's heart. This, of course, is done in every physical examination in a doctor's office. So if this were something that these people were just dreaming up, would not someone say the aliens got a stethoscope and listened...?'

A few weeks later, as reported by the *Daily Mail* (31 October) Jacobs was in the thick of it again defending his course on the subject taught to seventy-five students at Philadelphia University. There seems to have been quite a battle to get the matter on to the syllabus but Jacobs' objectivity was praised. The chairman of his department, Professor James Hilty, called the work 'important' and noted that as long as his colleague retained his open mind he would be supported. As Hilty pointed out, 'people didn't believe Copernicus either'.

This is all true. I find both Hopkins and Jacobs to be serious, honest and as far from cranky as you can probably get. But I feel the American perspective on these matters is rather blinkered. About 75 per cent of all cases come from there (way too many) and so its 'norm' (small, grey-skinned alien medics) is prematurely imposed on the rest of the world.

There are those who profoundly disagree. Philip Mantle, PR officer of the British UFO Research Asociation, created a stir when he announced prior to a conference at Sheffield that he had lost faith in aliens. The *Mail on Sunday* (9 August) reported on a 'close encounter of the vanishing kind', citing him as saying that when he began his involvement in 1979 'I was convinced we were being visited by aliens. Now I am not ... I can see no evidence at all of extra-terrestrial involvement.'

Dr Jacques Vallee, a computer scientist from California's 'Silicon Valley' is another respected UFO authority who challenges the alien interpretation of these stories. In *MUFON Journal* (June 1992) he pointed to some of the real difficulties with the alleged medical examinations carried out by the aliens. For instance, he questions the plausibility of the witnesses' experiences, even identifying emotions displayed by entities that have no trouble breathing our air or speaking our language, including all its idioms. He also feels that the genetic sampling methods used by the entities are too akin to those we might adopt in our laboratories. An advanced intelligence would almost certainly have a better and more efficient means of gathering the data than abducting humans piecemeal from their cars and beds and repeating the same painful medical probes upon them. Vallee, who in 1992 produced a controversial book, *Revelations* (Souvenir), also reiterated his views at the 'ET or not ET?' conference in Manchester during April and stresses that he is not terming the extraterrestrial theory absurd. Rather he is proposing that it needs to be modified and restated.

An attempt to do just that was made by William Bramley from San Jose in the *Journal of Scientific Exploration* (Vol 6 No 1, 1992). He tried to remedy Vallee's difficulties with a new evaluation of the extraterrestrial theory, suggesting that aliens might 'be capable of manipulating atomic and molecular bonding to a remarkable degree; i.e. that it can take a solid craft and the entities within it and quickly transform them into something less solid.' He also reminds us that aliens might be in a co-existent world which we only dimly perceive during infrequent interactions, rather like intelligent sea-living species would struggle to comprehend man's land-based society.

The Roper Poll

Undoubtedly the most astonishing event of 1992 was the unexpected results of a public opinion survey carried out in the USA by the Roper organisation. This prestigious body conducted interviews with almost six thousand people about alien abduction claims; much the largest sample ever taken. The results were then annotated and discussed in a document carefully titled 'Unusual personal experiences: An analysis of the data from three national surveys' and sent free to 100,000 health professionals across America. These ranged from psychotherapists to MDs. David Jacobs, Budd Hopkins and Ron Westrum, a sociologist from East Michigan University, contributed to the dossier.

Questions on the survey were well phrased and included a 'trick' response to gauge bias. Participants, unaware of what they were describing, were asked to say if they had experienced things such as small balls of light in their bedrooms, flying or floating sensations and unexpected periods of time missing from their recall, all identified by researchers as commonly described symptoms of possible alien contact potentially buried in the subconscious mind.

Although some questions really tested for a whole range of paranormal phenomena (for example 18 per cent said they had awoken feeling paralysed with a sensation of a presence nearby, which might fit apparitional encounters as well as alien contacts) the numbers that seemed to offer strong suggestions of hidden alien contact were still beyond expectation.

A key indicator was for those who scored 'yes' to four or more of these questions. Some 2 per cent did so. If such figures are extrapolated to the population of the USA it would come to 3.7 million people. If similar results applied in Britain it would mean 1.1 million secret victims. As these countries have around six hundred and sixty investigated abduction reports respectively such fantastic numbers, if they are to be taken at anything like face value, imply that way over 99 per cent of all alien contact percipients are never being discovered or researched. There would be a virtual epidemic of horrific proportions that has largely gone unrecognized. Of course, there are any number of reasons why this study might be misleading. But it still must imply there are a lot of hidden cases.

The impact of this survey soon took effect. Several of the practitioners who had been sent the document recognised cases from their own files that they had taken less seriously than these results suggested they ought to have done. Some began active research work. The future spin-offs may be dramatic.

The disturbing consequence is that this will only serve to polarize future abduction data more and more towards the USA pattern. These cases are already so influential on society worldwide (three US abductions have become widely-aired movies or television mini-series since 1989) that the rest of the planet is being forced into a trend it might not have followed without such overkill. Indeed, as my 1988 book *Abduction* (Hale) goes some way to illustrating, there are excellent grounds to suspect the global pattern would have been different and there would have been more variety had there been less influence from this massive set of American cases.

Sadly, whilst the possible 3.7 million alien contact victims in the USA have a good infrastructure to turn to, with dozens of psychiatrists, psychologists, doctors and sociologists freely researching the matter and taking on patients as part research and part therapy, the same is far from true in Britain. If the figures are correct over one million victims exist here but there is not a single medically qualified practitioner doing any sort of systematic research and only very sporadic efforts by anybody doing anything much at all.

This creates significnt problems. BUFORA received a case from a couple in the Quantock Hills of Somerset during 1992. They claim that the husband saw a UFO close up and was irradiated by it. He has since had abduction-like memories and claims horrendous physical responses to these. Investigators Ken Phillips and Judith Jaafar who initially explored the case were horrified by the state of the witness and the matter was debated extensively by the team of investigators that I coordinate, trying to decide what we should do in response. We are simply not qualified to make medical judgements as to whether this is a case we should, or should not, be involved with and the witness alleges that the medical profession has shunned him, interpreting his 'ravings' about aliens as evidence of some illness which they have been unable to properly diagnose or treat. Regardless of rights or wrongs in a case like this, the very fact that we have struggled for months to find anybody willing to take this poor man under some sort of care and try to help him – which has to be the primary objective of anyone who meets him – rather makes the question of whether he has 'really' had an alien contact an irrelevance.

The difference in attitude between the two cultures is most

clearly emphasized by cases such as this. In the USA the man would have had immediate access to doctors and other professionals who would have judged what to do and how to proceed with the twin aims of alleviating the symptoms of severe trauma and stress that he is undergoing, and probing his story to see if any meaningful data could emerge. More than likely regression hypnosis to the dimly recalled 'experiences' would have been conducted to develop the case and compare it with others.

At the end of the day it is not clear where this would have taken us. One more strange story would have been added to the growing pile. We would be no nearer knowing whether we had created a pseudo-memory from these experiments or helped coax one out that was already there. As to whether the victim himself would be better or worse off is anybody's guess; although the person would at least have felt that somebody qualified to do so was actually taking an interest.

In Britain, without medical support, with witnesses like this branded as 'ill' by practitioners who have almost certainly made no first-hand studies of the available data, even if they know that any such data exists, and with floundering UFO buffs way out of their depth trying to balance doing nothing against doing something they have neither expertise nor right to attempt, the result is that no progress is made and the victim receives no assistance whatsoever.

Neither position is ideal, but in a caring society it seems to be important that somebody with the appropriate skills at least be on hand to offer compassion. So whatever the problems the American approach creates at least their victims do not face such frustrating inadequacy. Britain and, to be fair, many other countries not alert to this sweeping phenomenon of alien contact, owes its victims more than total inactivity and empty pontifications about it being 'all in the mind'.

The MIT symposium

In the wake of the Roper poll an unprecedented event occurred at, but not sponsored by, MIT (the Massachusetts Institute of Technology). This at least rivalled NASA's Columbus project for the most significant contribution to alien contact study during 1992.

Using sums of money generously donated by anonymous benefactors, Dr David Pritchard (an MIT physicist) and Professor John Mack (a world-renowned psychiatrist and professor at the Harvard Medical School) helped to coordinate a most extraordinary five-day symposium staged in June, at this delightful spot just across the Charles River from Boston.

This was very much a working event. About 130 researchers, many medical professionals, some abductees, and a sprinkling of long term investigators came together to dissect the abduction experience in the most introspective fashion ever attempted. The entire phenomenon was covered systematically from how cases are discovered, through all the stages of the encounter, on to ways to help victims adjust to life within society. Invited participants were then asked to submit newly researched papers, with the emphasis on clinical results, covering as many aspects of these sub-divisions as they chose. These were then vetted by a committee of academics who approved the ones to be formally presented and allotted very strict time-limits for the presentations. Some papers got just three to four minutes, none got more than about twenty, such was the pressure of time!

All those who attended had to sign an agreement not to publicly discuss the detailed outcome and to let the proceedings of the symposium stand as the only record. This was to give freedom to allow open debate and ensure that the written papers (to be published) could have a more formalized air to them; although much of the lively discussion was, if the speakers approved, also to find its way into the proceedings. As I write, these papers are still to appear, but are expected to hit the medical and UFO communities with a vengeance sometime later in 1993. They are likely to be around half a million words long, I suspect, and will undoubtedly prove the starting point for any future research into these experiences and form the seminal work in the field.

The original intention was to make the symposium a 'closed shop', not inviting the media or even alerting them that it was happening. In this way some scientists doubtful of associating with an event that might be prejudged in tabloid terms of 'little green men' might be tempted to take part. As it happened this ideal soon failed and the news was broken, to the point that some stories appeared both before and after the event. Consequently I feel less constrained by silence than I once did, even though I shall respect the promise I made to Pritchard and Mack and comment only on general trends and things I reported at MIT myself.

The main source of this leak appears to have been the *Wall Street Journal* (15 May) which referred to 'trauma relief' on offer and, in its headline, how 'extraterrestrials play rough but John E Mack heals new "war of the worlds"?' Aside from that the report was fair enough, quoting Mack as saying that as a Pulitzer prize-winning psychiatrist (earned, it seems, for his psychoanalysis of Lawrence of Arabia) he was convinced this spate of abductions was not 'mass hysteria' and that witnesses 'have no reason to lie and come forth with great reluctance'. The latter statement in particular is one I can generally verify from British cases.

The scattered stories after the conference came from the few reporters carefully allowed in to protect the integrity of the event. That said, one left his entire book of detailed conference notes on a park bench; Keith Basterfield and I found it many hours after everyone had gone home by something of an amazing coincidence. It would have been a godsend to the *National Enquirer* or *Sunday Sport*!

These stories focused on generalities, restricted by their inability to quote what anybody said. Usually they paraded researchers expressing belief that something extraordinary was going on, countered by more sceptical psychologists who pointed to the fallibility of hypnosis as a source of accurate memory. Richard Boylan, a psychologist from Sacramento, made the point (of which I am very mindful) that it is easy for researchers to use a case to extract data and leave the witness high, dry and suffering. At times, I agree, there is a risk that the strain imposed upon a person can come more from investigating humans than aliens.

I presented a detailed statistical analysis of the British abduction data. The small, bald, grey dome-headed aliens so dominant in American cases have only surfaced in Britain in any numbers since 1987, when books from the USA began to appear. Formerly, British aliens were commonly of normal or tall height, with blond hair and Nordic appearance. They had less abrupt manners and engaged more rarely in medical examinations; although some speculate that British research, lacking much, if any, hypnotic regression, often only uncovers a surface layer or 'screen memory'. These more pleasant images obscure the real contact and its more traumatic content that is only prised out by repeated hypnosis sessions.

I also reported on two experiments. In one of these I asked a group of ten UFO-aware people (such as investigators) to fantasize an abduction in a relaxed (but non-hypnotized) state. Their stories had some features matching real cases. But a group of ten people who were not in any way associated with the field, had never read books on the subject but who had the same level of awareness as any member of the public would today from press, television and movies, came out with very different stories. These did not involve the small, grey aliens at all. Not one subject fantasized a medical examination or other key 'real' elements. Significantly, most of these people described the scene of being taken into the alien craft, usually the most dramatic part of any science fiction movie. Yet in real abduction stories over 95 per cent of all witnesses offer no memory at all of this transition. They simply 'jump' from being in their normal environment and meeting an entity, to being inside an alien environment about to undergo the contact itself. This pattern, which Eddie Bullard has termed 'doorway amnesia', is obviously crucial.

My other experiment reported on a personal regression under the guidance of Dr John Dale, a clinical psychologist, who took me back to a light-in-the-sky type UFO experience I had in August 1977. I should stress that I did not before, and do not now, believe that I was ever abducted. I do not know what the blue light was that circled a Chester field that night. Maybe an odd aircraft. But I realized that this starting point was similar to the way in which many abductions begin and wanted to have some opportunity to comment upon the process first hand.

Equally important was the chance to use this in a real UFO situation to test the accuracy of data retrieved from my subconscious under hypnosis. I had no conscious recall of things such as the day of week that the incident occurred or what I did before and after the events. However, I was aware of a source where all this information was recorded. So, under hypnosis, I could relive the episode, including whatever new details emerged, and test the information that came out. In abductions there is normally no way to judge the accuracy of newly retrieved 'memories' because the incident is fantastic and there can be no independent checks available. Here, whilst I could not make any statements about additional details I made regarding the blue light, I could give an absolute score on the accuracy of my hypnosis statements describing the day of week or activities before and after the sighting.

The outcome of this complex experiment was interesting. It showed that hypnotic testimony was sometimes able to facilitate real recall of events I had certainly forgotten. But just as often (the split was about fifty-fifty) I came out with information that was clearly fantasy because it was provably and totally incorrect. There was some indication that memories immediately connected with the incident were slightly better than those of unconnected things before and after, possibly because the incident itself was memorable enough to have been better recorded. But overall, the experiment showed without doubt that hypnosis was at best a hit-and-miss road towards any sort of truth about alien contacts.

That said, as I found from my sample of British data, and as was emphasized by several other papers from participants at the MIT symposium (for instance Keith Basterfield on Australian abductions and Eddie Bullard on American cases) hypnosis is only the main source of memory in about half the evidence. Stories which involve it little or not at all have no significant differences in pattern from those that do. A voluntary British moratorium on using hypnosis was operated by BUFORA for five years to 1992 but did not end the receipt of abduction claims.

Other research

Hypnosis, as just discussed, is often used as the whipping boy of this field. However, there can be no doubt that, for all its fallibility it is not the cause of the phenomenon, merely a dark glass through which it is sometimes observed. None the less, its importance means that work on its use must continue.

Dr David Gotlib, a Canadian psychologist, does an excellent job surveying the literature of his profession for relevant material and debating it in his publication *BAE* (the *Bulletin of Anomalous Experience*). In 1992 some of the gems he turned up involved hypnotic experiments. For instance, (*BAE* June) the use of 'abreaction' (the dramatic reliving of traumatic events under hypnosis) is clearly what is occurring in these abductee experiments. But in *Psychiatric Medicine* (1992) F.W. Putnam had shown how its use has ranged from World War I shell-shock victims to modern-day child abuse and post-traumatic stress syndrome sufferers. It has proved useful in the therapeutic treatment of these, offering hope that properly controlled it could also aid alien contact study.

On the other hand there are warning signs about over-reliance on hypnosis from problems with child abuse cases. Hypnosis is sometimes used to bring out repressed memories of this severe early life trauma which is thought to be creating psychopathic troubles in adulthood. But there is some evidence being unearthed by psychiatrists that at times this hypnotic work is generating 'memories' when none really existed, so as to let the subject subconsciously say what the hypnotist wants to hear.

Dr John Kihlstrom, a specialist in memory retrieval at the University of Arizona, pointed out that it can prove impossible to know whether stories that emerge are true or not. He spoke of how such work found this kind of memory very susceptible to what he called 're-invention'.

Dr Elizabeth Loftus, who has made a number of experimental studies of eyewitness testimony at the University of Washington, has found that it is not difficult to explore past memories with subjects and instill a totally fictitious memory of an added incident (such as getting lost as a child). Later, when recalling all their memories, subjects tend to include the false one, not realizing that it was fabricated during the study.

In *BAE* (October) Dennis Stacy offers a theory for discussion in which he links abduction memories with abortion. He seems to feel this new approach necessary because the startling image from the Roper poll of perhaps 200 million people abducted worldwide in recent years is 'simply unsupportable in terms of common sense and logic, including any imaginable need of non-terrestrial science or even the simple logistics that would be involved in such a fantastic undertaking.'

Stacy is, of course, quite right. But this does not explain what causes these alien contact reports. He points to how there has been an update on the abduction theme in the past five years, transforming the sexual elements that have always been present into a theme of 'alien/human hybrid babies' being implanted and extracted from female abductees. In American alien contact lore, post 1987, this has become the predominant reason for an abduction, but is almost non-existent before then and is largely absent in cases from outside the USA (although one British case is discussed in my book *Abduction* and predates even the American data). Stacy wonders if we might draw a parallel with the recent focusing on the abortion debate and whether the mechanism through which the abduction vision occurs might not have adopted this major traumatic theme as the vehicle to work out these human stresses.

In a way it would be somewhat like dreams being based upon personal experience. If a large percentage of the world fear nuclear holocaust, perhaps because of some global event like the Cuban missile crisis, then dreams of nuclear holocaust will at that time become widespread. If 'living dreams' are acted out in the abduction, possibly it also utilizes dominant imagery buried within our cultural psyche.

Case histories

In September 1992 I visited Hungary and discovered, not to my surprise, that abductions were occurring there. They were a new phenomenon, having surfaced only since books by Whitley Strieber, Budd Hopkins and myself had begun to appear the year before. They were also following the same pattern as in the USA, with the small, grey entities, and there was even a case of a woman who claimed impregnation, saying that a dome-headed baby had been seen on an ultrasound scan and then just vanished. Unfortunately, fascinating as such events are, they take us no nearer answering whether alien contact is a physical or visionary phenomenon.

During 1992 attempts to procure tangible evidence for these reports were made but, like the Budapest baby case and several similar recent events in the USA, absolutely no documented medical proof that a fetus was ever present and later disappeared has yet been obtained.

Another area of hope for the believers in the literal reality of these cases is the implant. In a few recent cases, certainly postdating the 1970s, witnesses say that aliens implanted some small device in their heads, presumably as some sort of monitor probe. Commonly this is put in the nose or ear via a long needle and is a tiny ball perhaps two millimetres in diameter.

Given modern technology such as CAT scans, these can be sought, although the only country where cases are taken seriously enough to make that possible (and where all bar two or three of the alleged implant cases come from anyway) is the USA. Here medical treatment costs big money and insurance companies are most unlikely to fund searches for alien probes stuck up somebody's nasal cavity! Equally, were such a case to emerge in Britain (and I know of none to date) it is easy to imagine the outcry if scant National Health Service resources were diverted from important medical treatment into such an uncertain investigation.

Unsurprisingly, cases of alleged implants have rather stalled. There have been some unconfirmed claims of sponsored research finding objects on scans at sites in their bodies where abductees say there should be something, but little hard data has been published in support.

One report is of an object discovered by an abductee in his home which was thought to be a possible implant that might have fallen out. Whilst work to interpret this tiny ball (a bit like cotton fibres) has not found a definite answer, experiments to analyse it have revealed nothing that absolutely shows this to have been an object of non-earthly design. Indeed they have not even conclusively shown it to be a manufactured object, as opposed to a natural ball of carbon material.

In Australia, researcher Keith Basterfield surveyed the cases (*International UFO Reporter* January 1992). He personally has a dental X-ray of shadows in the upper mouth behind the nostrils at a point where an abductee thought she had an implant. But the case has problems. A full face X-ray was later taken on referral from the original doctor and showed no abnormalities. Researchers suggest that in such cases the implant was 'removed' during an abduction between sessions. Such a possibility is unanswerable. However, an independent study of both X-ray plates by a highly experienced dental surgeon confirmed to Basterfield that, in this doctor's view, the 'implants' on the original X-ray were a consequence of the X-raying process, a sort of shadow effect. This is apparently difficult to spot. But, of course, it does not explain the coincidence of the 'implant' shadows appearing in a part of the body where the woman says she believed alien devices had been put.

The Manhattan transfer

However, undoubtedly *the* case of 1992 is an extraordinary and deeply debated affair which was first made public that summer. It has been termed the 'Manhattan transfer', for reasons that will become obvious. It divided American research and led to a plethora of underground papers circulated between key figures each offering counter-arguments.

It revolves around Budd Hopkins, a researcher whose honesty, from personal experience, I do not doubt. In April 1989 he had received a report from a woman who had undergone several abductions which she had only come to suspect after reading one of his books, *Intruders*.

Hopkins explored these claims with her under hypnosis, but they seemed to have ended in her mid twenties. Then, on 30 November 1989, he had received a call from this woman, Linda, reporting that she had had an even more frightening experience early that morning. She had literally been transferred from her twelfth-floor apartment in Manhattan, floated in mid air above the New York streets by the usual small, grey entities and taken into a room where she was medically examined. Upon her return (falling from mid air on to the bed) she was scared that the aliens had killed her husband and two young sons because she could not wake them, but a mirror held up under the nose confirmed that her worse fears were unfounded and that they were merely in a very deep sleep. They had thus experienced nothing of her nightmare kidnapping.

Linda's latest abduction was explored and added to the list. It would have gone little further but for a letter Hopkins received in March 1991 from two men claiming to be police officers. They said they had been living with a terrible memory and proceeded to describe having seen the entire alleged kidnapping episode whilst parked on the streets below. They had seen Linda taken into a craft, which plunged into the river and never emerged. Unsure whether she was alive or dead, missing or returned, they felt inadequate; their years of training had not prepared them to handle this situation. One of the two had spent nights parked outside the apartments trying to pluck up courage to go to the correct unit and find out if it had been dream or reality. He later had a breakdown.

Hopkins called Linda and told her of all this, warning her that the two men might visit. Months later she called to say that they had and had reacted in amazement when they not only realized that she did exist and was safe, but that she was actually expecting them to come, because she already knew Budd Hopkins.

Despite several attempts and some further letters and a taped report Hopkins did not meet the two men. They later claimed this was because they were not ordinary policemen but secret service bodyguards in a party taking a world statesperson to the heliport after a late night off-the-record meeting. Even more extraordinarily this VIP had seen the kidnapping. Indeed, it was speculated, the entire thing had been set up by the aliens for that purpose as this VIP, if he or she told this story, would go a long way to establishing the truth of alien contact to the world. It was claimed by several UFO journals in 1992 that this person was a top figure in the United Nations. Hopkins has not confirmed this allegation and when I discussed the case with him in June 1992 – before the above stories leaked out – gave no hint of this identity. Also calls to the VIP's office have produced absolute denials and the statement that the individual was at home in bed at the alleged time.

The case became even more fantastic during autumn 1991 when a woman wrote spontaneously to Hopkins. There had been no publicity outside a few private briefings within UFOlogy given in confidence by Hopkins, so this seemed independent corroboration. The woman was driving on the Brooklyn Bridge when all passing cars allegedly stalled. She then saw the abduction unfold in the streets below and some way off to the side.

Hopkins, David Jacobs, Keith Basterfield and I had lunch and discussed this case in June 1992. Both Basterfield and I were curious about the fact that the woman driver and the bodyguards, despite viewing the abduction from totally different perspectives, directions and distances (the bodyguards even used binoculars) both drew it to some extent with the same 'face on' perspective of Linda surrounded by the entities. As Hopkins is an artist I naturally bow to his superior judgement on what unskilled amateurs would do in a situation such as this and, to be fair, he took the comment on board and responded to it in his first article about the case (*MUFON Journal*, September 1992). He suggests that it relates to the poor artistic ability of the woman on the bridge and the superior talents of one of the bodyguards, plus quite normal errors of perspective made by people with no artistic training.

However, some disquiet was expressed by other researchers, notably because of the way in which every aspect of this case fell into the lap of Budd Hopkins and not any other investigator.

Having no first-hand involvement with any of the witnesses I am in no way intending (nor am I qualified) to suggest that this is a fabrication. I simply do not know the truth. But something which Hopkins called in a 1992 lecture 'the most important case for establishing the objective reality of abductions that I have yet encountered' must be treated with considerable caution as a matter of course. As the so-called 'case of the century' it has the potential to be either the biggest coup for this research field or its greatest disaster, should it be disproved. By that criterion alone one should check and double check every avenue.

A privately produced detailed 'reinvestigation' was circulated by three writers in the USA to various leading researchers. I am not familiar with these people or any motivations they may have for their work, but found some of their efforts to check the story were useful. They describe themselves as Joseph Stefula (a former special investigator with the US Army and an ex-MUFON investigator now resigned), Richard Butler (ex police and USAF security specialist, now a freelance researcher into abductions) and George Hansen (a parapsychologist).

They spell out their work in great depth but appear to have engaged in a freelance pursuit and suggest that the principal investigators of Linda's story have access to (still secret) data not available to them. They made enquiries at the apartment block but could find no evidence of any other witnesses. They noted that the loading bay of a newspaper is directly opposite the building and would have been in use when the incident occurred. Nobody there saw anything. They also checked with the heliport and claim no flights were on record during that night.

Of course, one might well argue around such things. For instance if the VIP meeting was a secret one the movement of key figures may well have been deliberately excluded from any log. However, the need for basic investigation such as this was, I think, undeniably justified by the potential repercussions of the case. Both Hopkins and Linda have now chosen to go public with the story and a book about it is, I gather, a distinct possibility. Therefore they must expect such sceptical attacks.

Any case that is strong will stand up to outside re-investigation. Nobody who willingly reports what they believe has actually occurred to them has need to fear nor, on the other hand, can they expect simply to be believed without question. Such a story must be subject to open debate.

Jerome Clark, one of Hopkins' closest friends, also a very serious and objective researcher and a man whose opinions I respect, has exchanged some diatribes with one of the self-appointed inquisitors of this case and responded well to charges that were (I think unwisely) levelled against him for what was fairly tacit support. In papers that were widely but privately circulated during 1992 Clark, I think sensibly and masterfully, makes various telling points. He notes that whilst the case is on the surface quite persuasive it is, despite the integrity of those involved, still subject to 'a number of serious reservations' and has elements that 'thus far defy satisfactory resolution'. He suggests that time be given for Hopkins to complete his study and that then outside enquiries could, indeed should, continue. Clark noted that, as editor of *International UFO Reporter*, he would be delighted to publish full debate that might allow the case to be 'eventually resolved to the satisfaction of all reasonable observers.' He added that 'Possibly the failure of both positive and negative analyses to address all the puzzling and ambiguous elements of the case has to do with the absence of one vital but missing truth, still undetected, which when found will tell us all we need to know.'

The same may indeed be said of the entire question of alien contact.

Ghosts

Ghosts are as old as the earth itself. We all love to scare ourselves with tales told in the dark as the wind blows evil-looking tree branches back and forth. But are these things simply pandering to a desire for entertainment and horror, or are they so popular because they touch a chord inside our souls?

A typical story reported during 1992 comes from Ernie Sears in Hampshire. On 14 June he was taking a friend's dog out for its Sunday stroll, leaving the house via the kitchen. As he walked past the small television set located in the room it switched itself on without prompting. He had vague thoughts about his deceased wife having returned to celebrate his birthday that day, but let them pass. In the afternoon Ernie went and sat in the garden to read and his friend stayed inside dozing on the bed. Suddenly she came out to report that as she lay there all of Ernie's birthday cards suddenly fell over as if knocked down by a non-existent wind. In addition, upon investigation, it was found that all his clothes that he had neatly laid out on the bed-settee had moved themselves mysteriously on to the floor. Apparently little things such as this persisted and Ernie seems happy to accept the idea that his wife was indeed making her presence felt from somewhere beyond this life, determined to show that she had remembered his special day.

Many cases revolve around small incidents such as these, of importance only personally to those involved but not necessarily of immense significance in the global scheme of things. Whether you can accept them as evidence that we have a spirit that stretches beyond the earthly veil must be very much down to individual interpretation. But clearly, on countless occasions such as these, many people the world over feel that something very strange is going on.

Rather more like a classic ghost story is the experience related by Malcolm from the Rhondda valley of South Wales. He was in his small basement bedroom of one of the typical terraced houses of the area taking off his clothes for the night. Aside from a candle flame the room was in darkness. Suddenly he sensed a 'funny feeling' and a 'sizzling or crackling which I both heard and felt … the hair on my arms and the back of my neck stood on end.' Having an overpowering urge to turn around he did so and there, on the wall, was a circle of white light within which was the black shadowy figure of a woman evidently staring right at him. At first Malcolm was, understandably, in total shock but when he got up courage he moved towards the figure. Despite the shadows he said that she was clear enough to recognize, had he known who she was. He saw wisps of hair, eyelashes, the way her head moved slightly back and forth and even the twitching of her lips. Reaching out a hand he attempted to touch the apparition, but as he did so the woman stepped backward and vanished, leaving only the circle of light on the wall.

Desperate now to find any rational explanation he scoured the room, hoping against hope that someone was tricking him. But he knew that the light had no source. He went to the window, confirming that the nearest light outside was far away across a railway track and, besides, thick curtains were draped across the window. Returning to the room, he saw that not only was the circle of light still there, but that the woman had returned. Steeling himself he walked right up to the glow and stood inches away from the wall and circle, trying to will himself to stretch out with both hands and see what he touched. If he struck the wall it would prove this was mere illusion, but he had an irrational belief that his hands would pass right through and he would be drawn into that 'other place' where the woman stood.

Malcolm finally edged his arms forward and yet again the woman responded quickly, stepping backward in clear reaction. This was enough. He fled the room and the house and spent the entire night sitting by a war memorial on a brightly lit street. When he did return to his house, next night, there was no circle, no woman, and they never appeared again.

Most ghost stories are unresolved ones such as this. We never find out who the apparition was, if of course it was anyone and not some trick of light and shade. We are left wondering if there might not have been some simple explanation. Even the witness himself, as here, eventually tries to convince himself it was a dream, but usually fails.

Of course, most old houses have some sort of 'haunting' associated with them. During 1992 ones that surfaced included the floating green mist or smoke that clings mysteriously to Bewsey Old Hall near Warrington, Cheshire, and said to be Lady Isobel Boteler from the fifteenth century.

However, it is less well known that ghosts are not always of human being or even animals. Ghosts of inanimate objects are by no means rare. Such a case cropped up in Sussex during 1992 and was researched by Diane Eakins.

On 8 May Justin Lycett was driving with a friend near a pub at Chiddingley where they had hoped to hear a band. As a musician he was happily chatting about this subject when something odd was noticed about the atmosphere. It was also unusually lonely. All traffic, people and sounds had vanished. This continued for some time and was considered most peculiar for a fine early summer's evening. Suddenly a reddish glow was noticed over the Downs in the Butts Brow area. Justin, who had some knowledge of aircraft, saw this resolve into a very low-flying shape akin to a Douglas Cargo plane. Intrigued by this unexpected sight, they parked the car and watched intently as it passed across the sky at an altitude of perhaps 100 feet. The oddest aspect was that it was totally silent, which was impossible for an aircraft of this size.

The aircraft appeared to have 'stalled' and was moving very slowly, on a steep downward path. Then, as if the pilot were fighting to save it, the nose reared upward and it turned towards them. They immediately switched the engine on and fled the area. Moments later they rounded a corner and met another car, and everything seemed to return to normal again. Sounds reappeared, the atmosphere was no longer ominous and the aircraft had disappeared.

According to the *Hailsham Gazette* (27 May) enquiries were made by the police and there was no record of any complaint about low-flying aircraft in the villages, despite the two men saying that it was heading straight for houses at Willingdon. However, there have been other reports of mysterious phantom aircraft in this same area. In 1991 one was seen at Seaford and Chris Emo from Willingdon later came forward to say that in early May 1992 he also saw a silent aircraft over Butts Brow, which might have been the same one.

During World War II there were several recorded instances of both Allied and German bombers crashing on these rolling hills. It is possible that somehow, sometimes, their images can still be witnessed.

Indeed Sussex is not unique; there were reports during 1992 of a strange aircraft seen to crash silently into the Mersey estuary off Bootle and there are other instances of the same thing, including a good daylight account of a wartime bomber seen to go into the waters of the River Dee estuary, precisely as one did in actuality during 1943.

Case histories

A case from the USA illustrates another aspect of ghostly experiences that seems to be important. They do not always involve people who are then dead, but are also very common in situations that are termed 'crisis apparitions'. Here the person who is 'seen' is undergoing some sort of extreme trauma at the time and, the theorists suggest, might somehow project an image across space to a location or a loved one with which they would dearly wish to connect at that precise moment: a kind of psychic distress flare.

Verda Kile from Garden Grove, California reported (*Fate*, September 1992) how after a tiring day and in the hinterland between sleep and wakefulness she suddenly had a strong image of a man frantically trying to prevent his car from crashing over a cliff. She could see and sense the despair as the wheels refused to engage and dig into the dirt and the vehicle was dragged towards catastrophe. Then she simply spoke out 'just let it go', because the link was draining energy from her, and she collapsed into sleep. She did not, of course, believe that this was anything but a dream or hallucination, so felt no guilt, but the mood of darkness persisted for a while afterwards until it lifted quickly and she felt a sense of freedom and happiness.

A couple of days later the news reached her that her brother had been found in his car at the foot of a cliff near Lancaster, California. The theory was that he had committed suicide, but Verda, remembering her experience, knew this was not so. She had not seen her brother for a very long time and they had only recently corresponded again. But she felt sure he had reached out to her in that moment of desperation. Later the police investigation vindicated her view. They found deep ruts in the earth and marks on the tyres consistent with the driver fighting valiantly to prevent it going over the edge of the 250-foot drop.

Psychic News (7 March) had another impressive case that offers evidence of something truly extraordinary. It was investigated by researcher Lynn Picknett. A family had moved into a new rural home near Canterbury, Kent and the parents were worried because their young son Mark had no friends in this area. He spent a lot of time talking to someone he called 'Albert', whom they assumed was an imaginary playmate that he had invented. But when Mark took to spending time by a disused well chatting to Albert they became very concerned, as this was a dangerous place to engage in fantasies. But Mark kept insisting that Albert was real and pointing into thin air, saying 'look'.

Then, one day, Mark's mother was peeling potatoes by the kitchen sink, her mind idling (a common trigger point), when she saw Albert too! At least, she saw a boy wearing very odd old-fashioned clothes standing by the well. She gripped the sink in terror but Albert, apparently seeing her, looked up, smiled and waved. Then he disappeared completely! Asking Mark for more details, his parents discovered that Albert had told him that he had lived in a cottage by a nearby pond but that this was now derelict. Making enquiries with a local historian it was found that there was such a place and that in 1913 a young boy had fallen down the well and died. His name was Albert Blackley.

After hearing a radio discussion by a psychic, the family decided to try to help Albert 'move on' and gently persuaded him to look for his own mother and 'move towards the light'. Since doing this neither his mother nor Mark himself saw or heard from Albert again.

Possibly the most common type of ghost story in modern times is the phantom hitchhiker or its variants. The most remarkable example of this category is a repeatedly seen apparition on Blue Bell Hill in Kent. For some years a young girl has been seen on this road by people passing by. When they turn around she has simply disappeared. A police inspector stopped to give her a lift once, fearing for a young girl walking alone. She got in the car, said her name was Judith and after a few seconds, when he turned to speak further with his passenger, he was alone in the car. She had simply vanished.

Speculation has been that she was a 22-year-old girl called Judith Lingham killed by a car on this stretch of road in November 1965. Top psychic Nella Jones, who has often given accurate information to police investigations, was called in as an experiment in late 1992 to see if she could find out why the ghost was still 'earthbound'. Prior to doing so she was misinformed that the 'ghost' had been run over by a car but she says that, upon arrival, she immediately realized that the woman had been travelling inside a car when another vehicle came down the hills, dazzling her with its bright headlights, and she had swerved to avoid a collision and then overturned at speed. Nella even offered details of the occupants of the second car, all of which proved correct.

Immediately after Nella's visit several local people claim to have seen the girl again, including Chris Dawkins of Coxheath, who late one night thought he had hit and run over a woman in a red scarf, but found nobody on the road when he stopped. Dawkins describes this 'ghost' in the way that most witnesses do, not as a transparent spectre or white floaty form, but as a solid individual. He was quoted by *Psychic News* (26 December) as saying the girl was 'solid – as real as you are … I thought I had killed her.'

There are now plans for Nella Jones to return to Blue Bell Hill in 1993 and attempt to help the estranged spectre find some sort of peace of mind.

Poltergeists

Unlike ghosts, poltergeists have a bit of a bad reputation. They are said to be noisy, disruptive spirits, rarely ever seen and usually just the cause of some mischief or other. Theories about them usually involve either wicked spirits marooned on earth or, from the more objective researchers, some kind of emotional temper tantrum somehow transformed from mental energy into physical energy and projected on to the environment in an unconscious fashion by a person undergoing stress.

It is not unheard of for council tenants to be rehoused because of trouble with dry rot or damp. These days councils also have to deal with a new complaint and sometimes move families on because of sitting tenants who do not have any earthly lease!

Kathyrn Meredith and her two children have had problems in their council house in Mid Glamorgan, Wales. It is built on the site of an old farmhouse and etheric traces of goings on there might still remain. Common difficulties they faced were having lights and other electrical equipment switching on and off by themselves. More terrifying was the cup that blew itself to a thousand pieces with a huge bang, slightly injuring the mother. The final straw came when Kathryn entered daughter Nicola's room and saw small bedside objects floating in mid air! At this she called a taxi and fled the house taking the children and, according to *Psychic News* (17 October), seemed intent on not going back.

A rather more unusual problem was faced by the Boulter family in Leicester. Their council house has been invaded by monstrous slime. It oozes out of walls and is coloured yellowy-white but hardens into a white residue. Whatever they do they do not seem able to stop it appearing. Priests have even been summoned. Electrical equipment has become so clogged up by this sticky, slow-moving goo that things like the video recorder and phone have malfunctioned. At times it drips down the stairs and other times all over the kitchen. The family's eight-year-old grandson has reported seeing an apparition in association with the arrival of the slime and calls it, without much evidence of fear, simply 'ghost'.

Samples were easy to collect owing to its frequent appearance, so these were eventually sent to Nottingham University for analysis. Although the family have no pets the liquid was found to be made up mostly of an unidentified animal urine. Both dogs and cats were ruled out, but this failed to explain where it came from. Mystery soakings such as these are surprisingly common in poltergeist outbreaks and in the past similar urine diagnoses have resulted from chemical analysis. However, nobody has managed to come up with any reasonable theory as to why such slime should appear at all.

As for the Boulters being rehoused, they do not want to be. They just want to get rid of the slime and retain their home. The local council pointed out that in any case it would be rather unfair to give them priority over homeless families. At least the

Boulters do have somewhere to live, even if somebody else is dying to stay there with them.

Research work

Paranormal investigator Tony Cornell from the Society for Psychical Research is waiting for an opportunity to test his new spider.

Spider stands for 'spontaneous psycho-physical incident data electronic recorder' and, whilst this monstrosity might sound like a prop from *Ghostbusters III*, it does have a serious intention.

The problem with photographs of ghosts is that they are all too rarely what they seem to be. In one case I have looked at, the impressive apparition in old-fashioned clothes in a Jersey castle was a display manikin reflected through two sheets of glass. Another was the camera strap dangling accidentally in front of the lens and so out of focus that it did look rather spooky. Another investigator described a case where the 'intruders' were not from another world beyond the veil, but unseen life-sized temporary cardboard cutouts of smiling people pointing the way towards the lavatories!

Cornell's box of tricks has a mixture of infra-red, still and video carmeras and can also simultaneously record things like temperature drops, sounds and changes in electrical fields. To overcome the problem of someone remembering to use a camera should a ghost appear, not as straightforward as it sounds when your jaw drops open and hackles rise, the spider will trigger automatically if something untoward appears and it can be left at a suspect haunted house for weeks or months waiting for something to happen. Hopefully, before very long this clever idea will pay dividends and, if there are such things as ghosts and they can be recorded for posterity, spider may be the very thing to establish that fact.

Meanwhile the intrepid Andy Collins, whose fingers are in many pies, was behind what he called 'Ghostwatch 92' – long before the BBC got the idea. His delightfully readable booklet giving an account of the proceedings is well worth your money. If you send voluntary contributions to ABC Books (Box 189 Leigh on Sea Essex SS9 1NF) you will receive a copy and the money you pay goes to the Rushton School for the deaf-blind and multiple handicapped.

Rushton Hall, in Northamptonshire, was itself the site of the ghostwatch expedition on 31 July 1992. It was precipitated, as is so much of what Andy gets up to, by psychic visions (in this case from his colleague Debbie Benstead). She had seen a triangle and led them to the 'Triangular Lodge' within the grounds of the hall and built as a folly between 1593 and 1597. To show how paranormal phenomena often overlap to a surprising degree, UFO contactee Gary Harlow (famous as 'Gary the alien' discussed at some length in my very first book – *UFOs: a British Viewpoint*, Hale, 1979) has himself often told me that this very lodge would one day prove to be of great significance because of discoveries that would be made there.

The decade-long visions of Gary Harlow and more recent ones of Debbie Benstead (which began on 23 April 1992) were only two of many from different psychics. Preliminary explorations revealed stories of a 'white lady' in the cellar areas and a party of several people, notably Andy Collins himself and colleague Karl Dawkins from the Earthquest research team, both saw this person walk past them on 10 May, describing the apparition similarly. As a result they confirmed with the proper authorities that a full-scale watch should take place.

A dozen people spent the night with auditory and camera equipment put together from sponsorship money. Some strange things were alleged during the hours of meditation, visualization and silence. The women in the party all felt the emotions of a female trapped in the area who had been badly mistreated. There were several fleeting sightings of her, and by 'tuning in' one group member claimed to have come up with information that was later found to fit in with a legend associated with the place. Even then it added to and corrected some details of this historical story.

Apparently several hundred years ago a local notary was reputed to have met an Italian woman whilst in Europe but left her and came home to marry. She had followed him to England and violent scenes had resulted. Later she died in the lake in the grounds, it was thought by her own hand. In this new version, however, she was strangled. All the women claim that they suffered the sensation of her death as the ghostwatch team tuned in to the affair and attempted a 'rescue', akin to that practised by the family in Kent when they 'sent' the boy Albert on to the afterlife. In the Rushton Hall rescue the participants focused on the woman and tried to 'coax' her 'into the light'.

Some resistance was met as she wanted to stay in the area awaiting her lover. But afterwards they felt that they had succeeded.

Of course, whether you regard this as true sensitivity to some real experience or creative visualization of a more imaginative nature must be your own interpretation. Sadly, despite the equipment that was on hand Andy Collins had to report that 'there were no physical manifestations, echoing the old belief that ghosts never appear when you want them to ...'

Meanwhile Dr Percy Seymour, who is an astronomer at Plymouth University, created a bit of a storm by coming up with a theory about ghosts. In fact, it was really just new clothes for an old theory, but quite eloquently expressed by the scientist. He told *Psychic News* (5 September) that all matter leaves a footprint on the material world which can be detected under the right conditions. His ideas stem from a realization amongst physicists that the separateness of objects is a man-made concept. This illusion is only real on the surface. When you probe deeper into the basis of matter everything is part of a timeless, spaceless, unity of order.

Seymour talks to what he calls 'world lines' that follow an object or person through its interactions with other things. His analogy is of a football match, which you can artificially slice up into thousands of 'snapshot' moments. During each of these the ball will be somewhere. If you then stacked these snapshots one on top of the other and put a dot where the ball was every time, you could draw a vertical, weaving thread to represent its motion along what would then be the world line of that ball.

If someone has a similar world line to that of another person or two lives cross or touch at some point then a rapport will occur. In life this might lead to crisis apparitions but as world lines are in a sense timeless and spaceless (at least in the sense we define these things) they also could exist after the point we in our earthbound mode might term death. In other words, if a person had strong habits, emotions or associations within a certain place his world line influence on that location might remain very strong. Someone who then crosses through it (perhaps by spending time at that place) may find their own world line coming into contact and experience the contact as a ghost. They would be touching the essence of that person outside our normal concepts of space and time.

Parapsychology

Parapsychology is the official name that scientists adopt when studying strange phenomena that are connected with the mind. We still know less about this unexplored region than we do about outer space or the deep oceans and only recently have we come to appreciate just what a pivotal role consciousness plays in shaping all human experience. Indeed, we do not even know whether consciousness is confined to humans (as a product of our hypothe- sized 'soul') or whether it is merely a natural result of electrical activity within the brain and so commonplace amongst all higher animals, although this second view is well supported.

The search for answers to such questions brings in a wide range of subjects, such as ESP, dreaming and all forms of unusual mental states which might point the way towards an understand- ing of inner reality.

In the USA some scientists, notably psychologists, choose to specialize in these areas of work. Consequently there are profes- sional parapsychologists based at quite a number of universities. The same is less true in Britain, although some researchers do work on parallel tracks and have clear interest in the field whilst doing mostly mainstream research. There are also a couple of grant-funded chairs of parapsychology, the most important of which is at Edinburgh University.

Psychologist David Gotlib reported on the fascinating study carried out by his fellow Canadians, Colin Ross and Shaun Joshi, which they published in 1992 in the *Journal of Nervous Mental Disorders*. This was, in fact, a highly useful sample of 502 adults from Winnipeg investigated in an attempt to ascertain the inci- dence rate of parapsychological phenomena within today's society. This is an important piece of data to secure.

They found, for instance, that déjà vu (the experience of having already lived through a moment of time) was remarkably common (54.6 per cent of the sample). As there are several less exotic

99

psychological theories that might account for it (such as misinterpreting the delay lag as data is processed from one part of the brain to the other) it may prove so prominent simply because this is a very normal, not supernormal, event.

A very interesting 17.8 per cent (nearly one fifth of the population if extrapolated) claim to have had a dream which included information about a future event that really happened and 15.6 per cent had had a form of ESP or telepathic contact at least once in their lives. Other well-scored responses were seeing a ghost (5.2 per cent) and some awareness of a previous life (4 per cent). Both these represent something like 12–15 million people in North America or around 2.5 million people in Britain who would profess that they had seen ghosts or experienced past lives, if the figures are extrapolated beyond Canada. The precognition and telepathy scores are even more staggering, being three or four times these numbers. It is, of course, difficult to defend continued rejection of, and lack of research into, an experience which a possible nine million British citizens might think has happened to them!

This experiment was actually set up to test a growing theory amongst some psychologists that experiences of an ESP nature are the result of a 'dissociative' process in their minds, effectively withdrawing from total absorption in real world events and 'tuning inward'. According to this concept it does not matter whether tuning in is to imaginative fantasies or real inner experiences.

This Winnipeg study found strong evidence that this dissociative factor was indeed very important. In the past it has been proposed that children who suffer trauma and abuse when young grow to adulthood with enhanced ESP claims because of their greater tendency towards dissociation. It has been reliably established that there is some substance to this claim and this new study again found a strong correlation. What is believed to occur is this. Such children in very stressful situations (such as being constantly abused) enhance the dissociative abilities that we all possess in order to 'escape' the horrific stress of the real world, which they cannot bear or even share with others. They may retreat into a fantasy world of their own invention (imaginary playmates are common in such children, for example). On the other hand, it cannot be disproved that they have access to information processed at the level of their subconscious mind as a result of tuning inward. The rest of us may simply filter this out. If such information includes ESP input more psychic experiences may quite naturally result.

The Ross/Joshi study found that the relationship between abuse, dissociation and psychic experience is not a linear one. There are many people who seem to have developed ESP and enhanced dissociation without any childhood trauma or psychopathology at all. So one is not the direct cause of the other. Childhood abuse may simply make it more likely that a person becomes psychic because it emphasizes learning processes which seem to facilitate that capacity, whatever that capacity is.

It is very interesting that this study closely parallels recent work on alien contact abductees. These people are also found to have more than the average level of childhood trauma and abuse, but again, not to the point that one must cause the other. Independently it has been proposed from such work by several American psychologists that there is some link between child abuse, trauma, dissociation and subsequent claims of alien contact – but it has not yet been proven to be as straightforward as that abused children go on to fantasize that their experiences were alien abductions. One idea is that they do this by hiding the sexual advances of family members under a guise of alien genetic experiments to make them more palatable. But, given the trauma of this sort of memory, and the fact that most abductees seem not to have had childhood abuse at all, this seems unlikely to be true.

In fact, abduction researchers pinned some hope on the 'fantasy-prone personality' hypothesis. This was based on work by several psychologists who had identified a specific percentage of the global population (up to about 4 per cent) who had strongly dissociative tendencies and as a result developed such a vivid dream and imaginative life that at times they had difficulty separating reality from fantasy in their waking memories.

Obviously, if such a person dreams of a flying pink elephant memory and consensus logic dictate that we label it a dream because we all know flying pink elephants do not exist. On the other hand, given the apparently similar claims by many other people, the reinforcement beliefs of active researchers into such claims, and today's cultural pressures making acceptance of them less difficult, if such a person were instead to have a vivid dream of an alien contact this might not be ascribed to the same clearly defined pigeonhole as the pink elephant. There could well be a far greater acceptance of the option that such a thing as alien contact might really have occurred.

As a consequence there has been quite a number of detailed surveys of abductees carried out in the USA, testing for fantasy proneness. Although there have been isolated cases found where an alien contact witness is strongly fpp (ie scores as fantasy prone) the general fpp score has argued against a blanket theory that abductees are so related. A three-continent cross-cultural study is under way in 1993 to try to answer once and for all whether there is any evidence that alien contact claimants are fpp, but none of the pilot studies look hopeful.

This work with such people has, however, thrown up other factors that emerge as a trend – notably amazingly detailed recall of very early life (well beyond the norm) and enhanced visualization abilities and artistic tendencies (often manifested as skilled artwork or poetry). These contactees are, therefore, creatively visual and this fact must be a key to an understanding of why they have the experiences that they do. Equally these people record a wide spectrum of ESP and parapsychological experiences as well as their alien contact, far beyond the normal level for society. This again suggests that the two phenomena may be related in some way. It also suggests that parapsychologists researching the dissociative tendencies of witnesses to psychic phenomena ought to search for these other curious patterns (such as the early life recall) that have been found independently by those who are researching alien contact claims.

Of course, many scientists find this work unpalatable because they assume none of this data can be in any sense real. But even attempts to disprove the status of ESP are important. One man who tried to carry them out was American magician and psychic showman James Randi. His television series (*James Randi: Psychic Investigator*, 1991) attempted assorted experiments to test things such as remote viewing and ESP. Throughout 1992 the fallout from this filled the pages of the *PSI Researcher*, an excellent scientific journal from the Society for Psychical Research.

In *PSI Researcher* (Winter 1992) Randi defended his work against charges made by Robert Morris, who holds the parapsychology chair at Edinburgh University. Randi has had a love/hate relationship with parapsychologists, many of whom do not like his challenge that they prove their case in a repeatable manner. On the whole I think that this is a necessary demand, even if it may ultimately prove impossible. For instance, if you were to try to demonstrate in a laboratory that A loved B (as opposed to A merely being biologically attracted to B, which can be measured in physiological ways) then it is very unlikely that any scientist could do it. Of course, most of us do not quibble about this inability to test this claim that love exists because, from personal experience, we simply accept that it does. Possibly one day a method will be found in which such an experiment can be carried out to order or, if love is a concept that depends upon abstract, undefinable things that can never be distilled in a test tube, it may well not be. Similarly, one day we may be able to come up with repeated tests that reliably prove some type of psychic effect. The fact that we have yet to do so simply shows that the task is difficult, not that it is impossible. It also suggests to me further evidence that it is emotion-led and consciousness-based, like love.

It is wrong of sceptics to say that a phenomenon does not exist until it is proven to do so under rigid test conditions, because these might unfairly restrict the way in which the process happens. Imagine having to prove you loved someone whilst wired up to EEG and ECG machines, with computers whirring and random number generators and video cameras firing on all cylinders. It probably would not help very much! But it is equally wrong of a parapsychologist to dismiss demands that we should try. For that is the only way we will ever discover if these things can be done or, if not, why they are impossible.

Therefore, I believe that challenges by people like James Randi, whilst often theatrical, are needed. In the past they have had a beneficial effect by showing it is easy to get carried away and not test your data as thoroughly as you should. On the other hand, Randi must stand up when positive results emerge. A couple of his television-based experiments did seem to lean towards that outcome (although most, undeniably, did not).

Randi resigned from the American sceptics group CSICOP (Committee for the scientific investigation of claims of the paranormal) because they were named as co-defendants in a case brought by Uri Geller who accused Randi of labelling him a fraud. Randi rather gleefully noted in *PSI Researcher* that 'the presiding judge has now ruled that Mr Geller must prove his claims of psychic power in the court room. I can hardly wait.' In the next issue of *PSI Researcher* (Spring 1992) a noted writer, the late Brian Inglis, disputed this and pointed out that in his view Geller's case did not revolve around proving his powers.

There was also more detailed disputing about some of the tests that Randi planned for his television series, and about whether claims for the use of 'rigorous scientific scrutiny' (words on the cover of Randi's book of the series) matched his own admissions in the text that an experienced conjuror could have evaded the prescribed security precautions.

In fact, Professor Robert Morris noted how one of the more successful experiments (where a dowser supposedly identified a single square in a blank map by dangling a pendulum over it) had flaws. To many viewers this was an impressive 'hit', but Morris argued that the procedure was seriously marred and Randi himself, whilst stressing that he was in no sense suggesting that the dowser cheated, had to make clear that the prop map noting the correct square had been left in the studio for rehearsals during a period when the dowser and other programme parti-cipants were already in the building. This seems to have been no fault of Randi's, but it does invalidate any hope that this seemingly successful experiment was a well controlled test. Others where the psychic did not succeed, of course, might have had similar drawbacks. This was, after all, presumably meant as an entertain-ing television show more than it was designed as a serious attempt to test parapsychological claims.

Some interesting new cases

In April 1992 Dr Keith Hearne, a well known specialist in psychic dreams, conducted some work at Birkbeck College, London, with hypnotherapist Lucien Morgan. This was really a prepara-tion for an experiment they intend to conduct in 'incubating dreams'. The process will involve taking people into a more natural state, getting them to fast and go through a psychological cleansing procedure, and then trying to incubate a series of unusual or even paranormal dreams. Apparently there are a number of ancient beliefs that such things work, when we free ourselves from the bonds of the excessively material world. However, some people seem able to do this spontaneously, either in a waking state or, more commonly, when asleep.

When 21-year-old Jo Ramsden disappeared in June 1991 a massive police hunt was focused on Dorset but to no avail. The case was made more poignant by the fact that she was a sufferer from Downs Syndrome. The chief inspector in charge of the enquiry, Alan Burt, noted that he was approached for months by assorted psychics, some well known and others just ordinary members of the public. They were offering advice, intuitions, visions and dreams that they thought might be relevant. Such a process goes on in almost every major disappearance or murder case, as if a tide of psychic ability is unleashed by the incident. However, police only rarely take notice of the material.

I spoke with John Alderson, who was the chief constable in charge of the famous (and still unsolved) disappearance of newspaper delivery girl Genette Tate during August 1978. She had vanished on a sunny day whilst on her rounds within a Devon village. No body was every found. From this I discovered the amazing number of offers of psychic assistance the Devon and Cornwall police received and how they ultimately chose to use this as a way to keep press interest alive so as to ensure that normal leads did not dry up.

In Dorset, by early 1992, Jo's parents were happy to accept any help to try to find out what had happened to their daughter. However, when Carol Everett put her psychic abilities at their disposal she was regarded in a similar light to all the others, a view she seems to understand the police must take. Carol held some of the missing girl's clothes and got clear impressions from these. She said that images entered her mind, and described these in detail. They included the fact that Jo was dead, that her body would be found soon in a wooded area and that the man who killed her lived locally, knew the girl and had even been seen by an elderly male witness who lived alone in woods north west of Bridport and who owned a black and white dog.

Several weeks after she made these statements some of them came true. Jo's body was indeed found and the location matched that offered by Carol Everett. It remains to be seen whether the other information that she gave is also correct, but this psychic cannot be accused of being vague or imprecise, as is the all-too-common argument when something seems to be successfully foreseen.

However, if this kind of work is by now almost routine the same cannot be said for the remarkable claims of London inventor Tony Bassett. Bassett told *Psychic News* (23 May) that he had, in effect, invented a time machine! In fact, what he had created, as a by-product of his interest in healing energies, was a small box that emitted electrostatic fields akin to those in the atmosphere prior to the appearance of a thunderstorm. Someone who lies with the box plugged in next to their head can absorb the emitted energy directly into their brain cortex and rapidly switch their state of consciousness. Then, through what appears to be a semi-hypnotic state, Bassett can 'guide' them out of their body and suggest that in this new freedom they can explore time and space.

Aisling Duffield reported how, using the time travel box, she found herself amidst the stifling heat of a jungle with an all sensory experience of being a man (perhaps visualizing a past life?). She was tapping latex sap from rubber trees. She described it as 'a kaleidoscopic dream' but said that she felt fully awake whilst it was happening. As an objective test the same woman was asked to 'drift' in this state a little nearer home and read the licence numbers on two cars a few streets away. These were then visited after the experiment and the numbers allegedly matched, seeming to suggest that she really was able to mentally travel in time and space as the creator of the box suggests.

Bassett believes from his preliminary experiments that travel into the future is also possible using this device.

It is intriguing that researchers such as Canadian Michael Persinger, a Laurentian University specialist in the effects of energy fields on states of consciousness, has long proposed that paranormal events occur because of a similar process. What he calls 'transients' (free-floating columns of invisible energy) can, he says, be met in nature and switch the state of consciousness of an unsuspecting witness, precipitating a strange experience. Perhaps Tony Bassett has created an artificial transient locked into a device and this can cause such changes to take place to order. If so then much could be done to develop research and try to discover why some people seem more prone to these spon-taneous experiences than others.

Another field in which interesting progress was made during 1992 was the subject of 'thoughtography'. This is the apparent ability to cause interference on celluloid by way of direct inter-vention of the mind, thus producing anomalous images on developed film that ought not to be there. The full scale process, where a recognisable image is simply 'beamed' on to unexposed film, has only been reported by a handful of psychics, such as Ted Serios in the USA. There have been no recent examples of the claim, but it does have a more common variant. Andy Collins conducted some research into this (reported in *Earthquest News*, Winter 1992) but he is only reflecting a curious trend which has begun to have impact in several fields, including crop circle studies and UFOlogy.

Several people in the past (Trevor Constable for example) have conducted experiments trying to film what they thought were 'energy forms' in the atmosphere. They appear as unanticipated dark masses on infra-red film, usually hovering in the air but never seen at the time. Attempts to explain these anomalies have continued but they still turn up from time to time on images taken at stone circles or other earth energy sites. Not uncommonly a 'psychic' or ESP-attuned person does the photography.

Constable's books (*They Live in the Sky*, 1958 and *The Cosmic Pulse of Life*, Spearman, 1977) are still well regarded by a hard core of people as fascinating research. But Collins became interested in 1979 when he accidentally captured a strange dark mass whilst photographing a UFO site in Clwyd in the presence of someone with strong ESP abilities. Nothing was visible but seemingly something was sensed at the time.

One of the few people to try to duplicate this work was Terry Cox, a very experienced UFOlogist, who over the years has produced a number of dark images from the Cornish countryside when nothing was visible at the time. Often the areas where the pictures were taken are those with a degree of legendary tales regarding 'spirits' or where something odd was 'sensed'. I briefly described Cox's work and included one of his remarkable photographs in my book *UFO Reality* (Robert Hale, 1983). I then asked photographically-experienced readers with any explanations to offer to come forward with these, but nothing emerged.

Andy Collins seems to think that Constable and Cox may have been photographing 'orgone energy bioforms' such as he has theorized might produce the crop circle patterns. It is therefore very interesting that a number of photographs taken inside crop circles have provided similarly mysterious images, although not usually dark blobs. More commonly they are streaks, orange smudges or white ovals. In fact, in the book *Crop Circles* (Robert Hale, 1990) there is a picture that Fuller took of a white blob in the spiral centre of a pattern. I had assumed it was something he had placed there in order to indicate scale, but when I asked him casually later it transpired that it was not and he had not noticed anything in the circle at the time.

Of course, the difficulty in situations such as this is that it is very easy to fail to notice something not of central importance, such as a bit of litter discarded or blown into shot by the wind, and when this is frozen *in situ* by the camera shutter it looks stranger than it might otherwise have done.

However, the sheer number of anomalous images taken at crop circle sites has now filled several articles (*Kindred Spirit* magazine featured some examples during 1992) and the number of photographers achieving these unexpected additions to their shots is now well into double figures. There have even been a couple of video films taken by camcorders sweeping across crop circle fields which have picked up small white blobs, similar in appearance to that in the photograph in *Crop Circles* and yet which move in a swooping, animated fashion, dipping into and out of the corn. Arguments about whether these are unresolved birds, small model aircraft known to be used by some researchers to attach a camera and take overhead views of circle patterns, or something else entirely raged throughout 1992. Most cereologists seem to prefer the view that they somehow relate to the mysterious energies involved at circle sites.

In his *Earthquest News* report Andy Collins discusses many other anamolous images taken in crop fields, particularly during late 1991 and into 1992 when these came to the fore. Certainly the choice is simple. Either they do reflect some sort of unusual energy concentrated in these locations or simply result from so many people taking so many photographs that the laws of average dictate that some must have flaws.

However, the process has also dogged the UFO field during 1992. Whilst it is common to receive images where the photographer says 'I saw nothing at the time but when I developed my picture there was a UFO on it', these almost always turn out to be film faults, drying marks on the negative, birds frozen in flight as they sail past the camera, or other equally prosaic solutions. But the same cannot be said for the photographs taken by Mark Glover, an investigator with BUFORA and the north-west group MUFORA.

Mark had investigated reports of a ball of light seen years before above the sand, rocks and beach area of West Kirby on the Wirral. On 11 August 1992, so as to round off his case file, he was taking a series of shots from the location on the sands, offering a panoramic view of the sky and showing the area where the object had appeared in 1978. Using a Polaroid camera and SX-70 film he developed the shots there and then. On five of the eight that he took in fairly quick succession, being those on the beach at the site, but with the camera pointing in different directions to minimize the risk of sun reflections, a distinct ball of white light formed in the sky. As Glover saw this effect emerge immediately before his eyes he could verify that there was nothing visible in the sky at this point.

Although nobody is getting carried away, least of all Mark Glover, who is a skilled and cautious investigator, there is no doubt that the images are intriguing ones. The pictures taken by the film immediately before reaching the rocky area and the last couple that he took quickly afterwards elsewhere so as to use up the film and act as a control all show nothing unusual. Only those taken at the location where the strange events that he was then investigating happened have this peculiar effect.

Conferences

Each year the latest results in the world of parapsychology are reported by the investigating researchers to a gaggle of conferences that are held at universities around the world. Here are some of the 1992 highlights from just two of these.

At the University of Nebraska in May Loyd Auerbach offered a fascinating update on work into psychic and lucid dreaming. Some of the experiments being conducted are intriguing. For example, it has been found that time in the lucid dream state is experienced at a different rate to 'real' time. It has also been learned that there is a whole spate of what are called 'night terror' experiences, where people awake in the middle of the night and claim that they feel paralysed with some force pressing down on them from above. For centuries these have provoked beliefs about 'demon lovers' and invisible presences. Today the same experience often triggers 'bedroom visitor' meetings with alien entities. However, new work suggests that this is in fact a semi-dream state so lucid that the person dreams quite realistically that they are awake. In truth they are still deeply asleep and the muscle paralysis is something we all undergo but never notice because it only occurs when we are too asleep to be conscious of it.

In one case in Canada a man claimed he had a vivid lucid dream of awaking from this state and jumping out of bed, irrationally driving his car, visiting some relatives and killing them. He had not been dreaming and had in fact committed a real murder, but he used as a defence the claim that he could not distinguish his lucid dream state from reality and, because he was actually sleep-walking within a lucid dream state, ought not to be held liable for actions over which he lacked conscious control. Whilst being sympathetic, some fear such a claim could set a frightening legal precedent.

Lucid dreaming is a field that has had to fight to gain a foothold in mainstream psychological research because it is often branded as 'psychic'. The dream state is so vivid and so precisely duplicates the bedroom environment that lucid dreamers can be unable to decide whether they are asleep or awake. Often when they realize they are asleep they gain some control over the dream and its lucidity is enhanced. About 20 per cent of the population have these dreams rarely, about 1 or 2 per cent quite regularly. From personal experience I can attest to the fact that they are amongst the most awesome and magical experiences imaginable.

Auerbach advises dreamers in a lucid state not to try the old advice of pinching yourself to test if you are awake. Apparently this does not work. However, if you decide to test the dream by seeing if you can float into the air this will soon resolve the question. Evidently some dreamers have attempted to fly out of a window. This is not recommended! But attempting to walk through a closed door or wall is less dangerous, if not entirely free of pain should it transpire that you are not dreaming. Of course if you are in a lucid dream state you will float, fly and pass through walls and doors without ill effect. To do so and 'wake up' to the fact that you are 'asleep' produces an enthralling feeling that knocks spots off virtual reality game machines.

Parapsychologists are currently trying to define the best ways to use lucid dream states to good advantage. There are techniques to help you learn to do it, if you have not experienced it, and it seems to be a good way to practise in a realistic but physically harmless manner things such as confronting a phobia or choosing between two future courses of action.

In the lucid dream state, Auerbach reports, psychic experiences do also seem to occur more often. A woman had a lucid dream that a friend went to Reno, had a car crash and died. When asked if she intended to go to Reno, the friend said she did, so a warning was given and she chose to stay at home. It is impossible to say whether she is alive because she did not go to Reno and so defused a precognition that might otherwise have come true, or whether the dream was never a true premonition in the first place and nothing would have happened even if she had gone to Reno.

However, of much interest to other areas of paranormal research is the recent discovery that lucid dreams can occur in a waking state. This seems to verify a suggestion that I made in my book *Sixth Sense* (Hale, 1988) where I proposed that nature decreed balance and a 'waking lucid dream' state must therefore exist. In a lucid dream the person is really asleep but then enters lucidity and has conscious control of the dream world which their mind has created. I suggested that in the mirror opposite waking lucid dream the person would be awake but would enter lucidity and there find they had some control over their waking environment.

In the lucid dream magical things seem to occur in the dream environment and yet you feel wide awake, whilst knowing that the vividity is simply part of a dream. In a waking lucid dream I would argue that magical things would also seem to occur, not in a dream environment but within the everyday waking reality of the normal world. You would also feel awake and conclude that you were awake because of the continuity of the normal environment rather than the immediate intrusion of a dream world environment that you invented. I think the waking lucid dream state is a very close analogy to the kind of half-real and half-visionary nature of many strange phenomena, such as apparitions and alien contacts.

Some evidence that this theory has merit emerged from studies conducted on victims of post-traumatic stress syndrome following the terrible earthquake that hit the Oakland and San Francisco area of California in October 1989. Several of those affected went through what were called by psychologists 'daymares', in which they relived, very vividly, and whilst completely awake, a version of the earthquake, being totally convinced it was happening again. Victims insisted that their houses shook and, utterly convinced they were awake and that a new quake was occurring, it only gradually became clear to them that this was a lucid dream within the waking state.

If this does point the way towards confirmation of my hypothesized waking lucid dream it may prove very significant that it was first recognised in a non-supernatural form amongst those diagnosed as suffering from post-traumatic stress syndrome. Some psychologists have already begun to find evidence that victims of alien abduction cases have a greater-than-average tendency to display similar symptoms. Of course, you might argue that this is an expected reaction to a real trauma (prior real abduction by aliens) which they have undergone and buried in their subconscious. But equally, the strong belief amongst many of these abductees that they have further abductions on a continuing basis may prove to be waking lucid dreams occurring as a natural side effect of the stress syndrome. If an earthquake victim suffers post-traumatic stress, has waking lucid dreams and 'lives through' more earthquakes, the non-reality of these can be clearly shown. Had a real earthquake occurred there would be no dispute. But if a victim believes they have been abducted and claims further abductions nobody would be able to prove these had not happened.

Meanwhile the prestige event on the annual calendar is always the Society for Psychical Research (SPR) convention, a body which has over a century of pedigree behind it. In 1992 this was staged at Manchester College in Oxford in September. One of the most interesting results, in a year otherwise disappointing for meaningful data, was an experiment reported by Howard Wilkinson and Alan Gauld. They had tested Persinger's theory of a link between electromagnetic radiation and anomalous phemomena but failed to duplicate his work in its entirety. But they did find some rudimentary clues that there was a pattern which deserved further study.

In addition, during August, the Society for Scientific Exploration had its first European conference, in Munich, Germany. It focused on 'anomalistic observations' and had a few sketchy papers on topics as diverse as UFOs, astrology and crop circles.

Research results

In the *Journal of Scientific Exploration* (Vol 2 no 1) computer specialist Dr Jacques Vallee reported on an old-fashioned experiment into psychic senses or PSI. He tested remote viewing with twelve subjects.

This phenomenon normally relies upon a technique similar to one that I used with a multiple test for the magazine *The Unknown* in 1986. Here a list of target locations were fed into a computer and a date and time announced in advance to readers who wished to take part. They were then asked to enter a state of reverie at the specified time and try to 'tune in' and describe what they saw. A computer programme on the day of the experiment selected the target area I was to visit and at the appropriate time I was thus at a place nobody, not even myself, could have predicted until just prior to the experiment. I recorded what I saw, smelt and heard at this location and the readers who took part tried to detect some of the essences of these from distances of up to hundreds of miles away.

Some quite intriguing results emerged; there was, for example, a graphic description of lock gates and a canal at one of the locations. White water was churned up on the surface by a passing freighter. Although one subject seemed to have got it completely wrong, offering an account of a pile of mashed potato, my site photographs taken during the test show that this subject exactly tuned into what was there. The water did indeed oddly resemble a pile of mashed potato but that had not occurred to me until I saw the photographs afterwards.

Vallee's 1992 experiment was different from this approach. His subjects all over north America each had a computer terminal linked by modem. What they had to do was use these to type in an instant description of one of ten selected mineral samples being viewed at the 'sending' location. Later a panel of independent judges matched the responses to what they thought was the correct sample, having no idea whether this was right or wrong in any case. That offers a way to overcome any subconscious bias and shows whether there really is an undeniable 'correctness' to a subject's description which matches the correct sample and only that one. This is known as 'double-blind' scoring. The results indicate that in eight from thirty-three runs the correct sample was identified by the description. This is twice the level predicted by chance and suggestive of some genuine mind-to-mind bridge.

This novel way of testing the phenomenon had many strengths but lacks the element that I think most important to the appearance or non-appearance of PSI. That is some kind of emotional motivation. If that can be built into a future modem-linked computer-based remote viewing experiment like this, perhaps extending the range between subject and sender from what was here an impressive couple of thousand miles to possibly all the way around the world (or even from a space mission back to earth) then this would be a fascinating and novel experiment.

However, possibly one of the least likely fields of research is something detected by Hilary Evans and given the name 'Slide', which stands for 'street lamp interference data exchange'. Believe it or not he is accumulating evidence about people who appear capable of affecting street lamps simply by being near them! In *PSI Researcher* (Spring 1992) he outlines why he has taken to the subject. It is 'an anomaly without a history' and so unlikely to attract as many people who are merely following a trend as other fields. Equally, it is so difficult to fake effects on street lamps (dangerous, public objects that few people understand) that any claims are reasonably objective.

Evans has begun to mention the effect on radio interviews or at lectures and cases have started to come in from all over the world. People seemed genuinely relieved that they were not alone in experiencing this curiosity, usually taking the form of a light switching off as they passed right underneath it and commonly on a recurrent basis which minimizes the possibility of chance. He now has over fifty examples.

Evans does not know if this is a unique event or linked to other possible phenomena in people's lives (are they, for example, affecting other electrical equipment around the home?). He has only just begun this research and is seeking further examples (see address, page 187). Now he realizes that the research must go further, seeking to verify the effect and find out what patterns there might be in the lives of people he has termed 'sliders'.

Theories

In the *Journal of the American Society for Psychical Research* (January 1992) Robert Becker reports on work to test the basis of human thinking processes. He is particularly interested in how they might be affected by outside magnetic fields, which might give some clue towards the nature of consciousness

Becker has found that only fields with relatively small local strengths, such as the earth's own geomagnetic field, seem to have measurable effects and that this supports a two-tier view. Most of the higher thinking processes occur when neurones in the brain cortex respond and fire, passing on messages across links called synapses. However, behind that seems to be a very different 'magnetic brain' which is perhaps a layover from less evolved humans and may well be more important in other animals. This is more responsive to electromagnetic fields.

Becker further suggests that PSI operates at this level and so is normally undetected by the conscious brain. However, if the flow of other information triggering neurone impulses can be reduced (as it may be by meditation or during sleep) then the 'magnetic brain' is more open to influence. At times when the earth's magnetic field is quiet this will not disrupt possible interaction and ESP-like phenomena may be detected.

The discovery that more receptive forms of PSI occur when there is minimal activity in the earth's magnetic field and yet less when this field is very active could prove vital. It supports the work of Persinger about PSI events being related to stimulating fields of radiation. Other discoveries in PSI research also match what Becker reports.

For example, the 'Oz Factor', something I first found in UFO contacts (but later in other areas of PSI) was reported in 1982. This seems to be an indication that prior to a person undergoing a PSI phenomenon the witness stops paying attention to outside sensory input. This is noticed most often by these people as ambient sounds disappearing, traffic vanishing off roads, birds ceasing to sing and an apparent isolation of the witness from the world about them. Different people have described this as being surrounded by a bell jar blocking out the outside world or suddenly 'turning inwards' prior to an experience, with both speech and thinking processes temporarily halted.

If Becker's discoveries are verified, what this may suggest is that such a process is needed to reduce the activity of the higher brain and the firing of neurones. Once the Oz Factor takes hold, the person has more direct awareness of their 'magnetic brain'. This, as Becker says, is far more susceptible to influence from any external radiation fields. Therefore a person in this primed state might detect an ESP message from another individual's consciousness field, tune in to a past-life consciousness field or even tap into a universal store of data in some enveloping electromagnetic radiation field, thus possibly experiencing either spiritualistic rapport or an alien contact, according to circumstance.

Perhaps this will open the door to a general theory of how PSI can happen that might also blend together many divergent paranormal phenomena. The boundaries of these are now recognized as being hazy at best, and have very possibly been artificially defined by ourselves.

Dr Serena Roney-Dougal added much to this with a report about her theories to the Society for Psychical Research in London in May 1992. She finds that the pineal gland, in the forehead area of the brain, is a key to PSI experience. This has long been the source of the mythical 'third eye' but new work shows that its actual function is to produce pinaline, a substance that inhibits the use of the hormone serotonin at the synapse links within the brain cortex.

What this suggests is that when the pineal gland is active serotonin will not flow quite so freely, thus perhaps causing a 'tuning out' of higher brain functions that are now prevented because the synapse links are no longer firing freely in the brain. In that sense pinaline flow from the pineal gland would seem to be a potential stimulator of the Oz Factor and may even be the physical basis for this psychological phenomenon. This phenomenon in turn seems to be the trigger that puts a person into the appropriate altered state of consciousness where they became more susceptible to ESP experiences.

The way in which these new research results gel with current advanced theories derived by different researchers from quite different approaches and examination of a range of different paranormal experiences may well prove to be very significant. At the very least it is an indication that although we have divided this book into sections discussing what seem like divergent paranormal phenomena we have often had to cross boundaries, because the results dictate that. There is a good case for arguing that the differences we impose may be more apparent than real.

This is a further reason why a book such as this was worth producing: to highlight such interweaving of the different subject areas. That ought to serve as a warning to researchers in any subject area not to ignore the possible value of other areas. I strongly suspect that the real answers will come from a much broader perspective on the way the paranormal operates and that patterns between such events will prove critical to any general theory that results.

Psychic Questing

To some people the pursuit of psychic questing is little more than a group of grown-up adolescents involved in a rather more sophisticated role-play fantasy game, a bit like 'Dungeons and Dragons' in spacesuits. But it has taken on a strange role within paranormal research and has now both its own growing literature and army of adherents.

In *UFO Brigantia* (51 & 52, Spring & Winter 1992) Clive Potter and David Taylor attempt a detailed assessment of the field, tracking its relatively modern history but illustrating that it does have antecedents going back much further than that in the spirit medium world. As a field in its own right it is possible to place its origins no earlier than 1979. In that year a group of UFO investigators working together in a small Midlands team called 'Parasearch', notably Andy Collins (again!), Martin Keatman and psychologist Graham Phillips, became involved in a case that I was researching. This concerned a family from north Wales and the various strange phenomena, from premonitions to alien visions, witnessed in particular by their children (see *Alien Contact*, Coronet, 1983).

Although I did not know it at the time (being given only hints that something 'big' but undescribed was happening) these investigators, members of that family and a whole host of psychics they were in contact with all began to receive messages about the need to find an object and do something with it. They pieced these together like a jigsaw.

Questing thus became defined as putting together clues obtained from paranormal sources of information and trying to understand what they implied. Then, rather like a treasure hunt, using these clues alongside maps and other more normal accompaniments to scour the countryside, the questers began a search for artefacts, such as buried swords and stones. In effect it was to become not dissimilar to the mythical King Arthur's search for the Holy Grail but set in the context of a hi-tech world and against a background of psychic messages, seances and precognitive dreams. Questing metamorphosed into its own field from a combination of earth mysteries, parapsychology and UFOlogy.

That first quest spanned months and eventually led, it is claimed, to the discovery of both a small sword (with an inscription using the words 'Meonia' and 'Mary') and, using that as a guide, a small green stone like a smoky opal. The team then had to charge this with energy at power sites such as stone circles and fight some sort of cataclysmic battle against the (unseen) forces of darkness.

Supposedly the sword and stone had long traditions (although the sword was found to be a Victorian copy) and a team of people similar to this modern band of questers had possessed both through the ages, including, at one point, Mary Queen of Scots. Their rediscovery today was believed to be merely the start of a longer process. Other objects had to be traced and brought together. There was an air of millenialism and a fever about all this, with a deep stratum amongst the paranormal community arguing that as the year 2000 approaches some kind of great evil will descend upon the earth and must be fought.

This original quest was written up in 1983 as a book called *The Green Stone*. Along with a later softback edition (Grafton, 1985) this went on to pick up quite a reputation amongst the new community of questers and would-be questers gathering together. The authors of this first book and a later sequel (*The Eye of Fire*, Grafton, 1989) were Martin Keatman and Graham Phillips. The latter told of subsequent quests and the discovery of a red stone, although there was much more that (as yet) these authors have not published, and I gather several further stones, with different properties, were traced.

My involvement in questing is almost nil, something misunderstood because I wrote the foreword to *The Green Stone*. I did this merely because I knew all of those involved, accepted their honesty and felt this was the start of something interesting. At no point had I been told about the various nocturnal missions around Britain and only later did I see any of the artefacts myself. The only (very minor) instance of any personal involvement was that I did see three white lights line up into a triangle over the Avebury stone circle when passing there in

September 1980. I tried to rationalize what I saw as parachute flares (which it may well have been) and only much later was to be told that the questing team had been sent to charge 'the third light' into their green stone by taking it to this very same ancient site.

Coincidence or not, I was obviously intrigued by this and by the appearance of a series of hugely popular novels by American fantasy writer Stephen Donaldson which had some strange synchronistic links with the real quest. These (for me) stretched coincidence to the limit. There is little doubt that the quest team did not know of Donaldson's then very embryonic stories, nor he of that team or its work. His original novel merely seems to have expressed an idea that had found its time within human consciousness (a sort of psychic parallelism). As the real questers toured Britain in their hunt Donaldson's *Chronicles of Thomas Covenant* were producing their own form of cultural tidal wave. A lot of people were deeply affected by both, but particularly by Donaldson's immense novels, which eventually spanned millions of words, and became global best-sellers.

Andy Collins had not been a co-author of either Keatman/ Phillips book but not, he stressed to me, because he disputed any of the events described in them. Nor did he opt out because he doubted what he himself had witnessed. I think he wanted to take a different approach to presenting the facts. The two Keatman/ Phillips books do undoubtedly suffer from an element of drama-tization of what took place, to the point where it became easy for people just to assume they were fairy tales presented in the guise of fact so as to make them sell better. I do not believe this, nor have I ever thought questing is anything like as simple as that. But I do fear the style of *The Green Stone* and *The Eye of Fire* did not help endear the field to the rest of the paranormal community.

Andy Collins bided his time and, in my view, acted sensibly and in a way that I respect. He conducted masses of historical research, perfected his writing skills and continued the questing work after 1979. He gave up UFO research and organized regular conferences in London, launched *Earthquest* magazine and his own publishing company (ABC Books) whose efforts were frequently superior in quality and appearance to many longstanding and big-budget publishing ventures. ABC Books became the vehicle for Collins' prolific output of ideas which have rightly earned him an excellent reputation within the research community.

He published a small book describing his own version of the green stone affair, entitled *The Sword and the Stone* (ABC Books, 1985) and his most controversial work of all, *The Black Alchemist*, (since republished as a 1992 Century Arrow paperback.)

The Black Alchemist tells, in a hard-to-put-down fashion, a story many will find equally hard to swallow. It purports to offer the results of a knowledge quest and battle against some sort of invisible foe, fought around Europe in 1986 and 1987 and culminating in the great hurricane of 16 October 1987, which devastated much of southern England and also caught weather forecasters off guard. The reason, if this book is to be believed, is simple. It was a kind of psychic weapon unleashed by the 'baddies' in the war of good versus evil.

Also in 1992 Andy Collins produced his magnum opus, *The Seventh Sword* (Arrow). This is a much expanded, indeed very lengthy, and yet wonderfully readable, account of much of questing history from the time when he checked out the *Alien Contact* story thirteen years before to the position today – with a team of psychic questers having found no fewer than six near-identical 'Meonia' swords and being hot on the trail of the seventh, and supposedly final, one. The book was meant to get the public at large involved in this search for that missing treasure.

It is easy to see why this extraordinary blend of historical research, role-playing, paranormal data gathering and adventure should polarize opinions as it has. Even within the paranormal research community you will find as many critics, who think it all a sort of belief-inspired fantasy, as you will those who regard it as more vital than any other supernatural phenomenon currently taking place. And, of course, the questers themselves point to the hard evidence they possess in the form of retrieved artefacts which at least makes their field more tangible than some where physical evidence is almost non-existent.

Even amongst questers themselves opinions vary quite widely on what all of this means, from those who see themselves as playing a pivotal role in guarding our future against real evil to those who seek some sort of rational explanation, even if exactly what that is eludes them.

Potter and Taylor term questing a sort of 'psychic whodunnit' which is 'repackaged to suit the current "New Age" climate, brought up on "Star Wars" and "Lord of the Rings" ... ' Indeed questing itself does resemble a cross between those two classic fairy tales of the twentieth century and may emerge from the same well-spring of consciousness, whatever its source proves to be in the first place.

The events of 1992 in the questing world were quite dramatic. Most specifically the seventh sword was announced as having been found. In fact it was found before Collins' book, *The Seventh Sword*, was published but it was decided not to change the structure of the text at a late stage as it 'might ruin the publicity theme of "where is the seventh sword?" ... ' that the publishers were adopting.

As far back as October 1989, on the tenth anniversary of the uncovering of the first Meonia sword at the Knight's Pool deep in the south Midlands countryside there were strong psychic images that another would be found in the same place, possibly even buried on the other side of a stone bridge, just as the first sword had been prised out from behind crumbling stone where it was supposedly placed a century before.

After many adventures the team had uncovered 'three keys of balance' from sites in Yorkshire, North Wales and Somerset. Collins outlines the saga (in the true Norse sense of that word!) in *Earthquest* (June 1992). He tells how St Bega 'had been our guide on the quest' and caused 'one of the most dramatic apport appearances I have ever been witness to in my career as a psychical researcher.' (An apport being a sudden manifestation of an object arrived out of nowhere, seemingly teleported from somewhere else.) This turned out to be a gold ring that 'appeared amidst a burst of light' falling out of thin air at a cross in a churchyard in Bassenthwaite, Cumbria.

After many other trips and historical probings back to the Middle East, Sumeria and the Egyptian time of Akhenaten (long believed by the team to be the point from which the artefacts supposedly first came to Britain) the last sword itself materialized in a most amazing fashion. In fact, Collins was called by an antique dealer who had purchased it from a store some miles from his patch. That store had been selling it for a couple of days, having picked it up from a house in Essex. Incredibly, the store where the seventh sword had been on display was in Leigh-on-Sea; as Collins says, 'just 880 yards from my very home'.

Following this discovery (on 24 July 1991) the team that had been together for so many years suffered what Collins terms 'differences of opinion' and went their separate ways as if their task was completed. They did, however, 'authenticate' the sword which, it seems, is older and heavier than the earlier copies and may date from the seventeenth century.

The news was kept quiet for some time but in 1992 it was decided to come out into the open and, what's more, bring the Meonia swords together for a ritual meeting. The cover of *Earthquest* (Winter 1992) thus has a unique photograph of all seven similar-sized hand swords embedded into the earth, symbolizing the end of the quest – or, as some people clearly believe, merely the end of phase one of the quest. What happens next is anybody's guess.

Of course, how you interpret these astounding events is a personal matter. Some will accept them completely. Others will prefer a more allegorical acceptance. No doubt some will find it impossible to regard questing as more than a gigantic hoax. But, if it is, a lot of people have now been sucked in and it is hard to see how the pretence could have been maintained for so many years.

In fact, lest you think the veracity of all of this rests in the hands of just one small team, I should point out that two of the swords were found by completely independent people, Colin and Gelly Paddon, who found them without any knowledge of or interest in the Meonia quest or the legends associated with it. They simply appear to have discovered them by strange coincidence in August 1985, an event which did produce some publicity at the time and alerted quest members to the discovery of what turned out to be swords two and three in the seven sword sequence.

Andy Collins organized a ceremony at a secret location in the Malvern Hills in August 1992 and Gelly Paddon came from Canada to bring her swords. Others who found swords but are within the questing fraternity were also persuaded to come along with their charges so that all of them were in one supposedly 'primed' position. It seems that nothing dramatic took place at what was largely a symbolic affair. Indeed, there is a feeling amongst some questers that it goes very deep and that the purpose is to build a bridge between the consciousness of humanity and the energy forces that lie *in situ* at these ancient sites. As a result a shift in cultural awareness may come about.

Andy Collins warns that there is much that has never yet been told and that some of this will 'kick down the very doors of established reality.' He also makes plain that 'the Meonia story has no way ended.' Few who have followed this story would doubt that.

Survival

Possibly the greatest question that anybody can ever ask is 'what happens after we die?' It is so profound simply because it is the one big unknown that we must all face up to. We can go through life never experiencing, caring about or pondering subjects such as UFOs, ESP and crop circles, but we cannot avoid death. Apart from birth it is the one experience that every single person must eventually share. Not surprisingly it has taxed the minds of the greatest thinkers since homo sapiens developed consciousness. Remarkably, almost every culture ever known, from tribal societies on a remote island to great empires like the Greeks or Egyptians, all believed in some aspect of the self which survived the extinction of the physical body.

Why this viewpoint is so prevalent remains a mystery. The common option of science is to term it wishful thinking or the mind's way to obscure the inevitable, but if we are merely a biological computer as this position implies then the concept of survival would be redundant. Computers have no need to ponder what happens when you press the off switch. If we are dictated by laws of evolution the very fact that every single being from neolithic times to the space age of today has this sense of personal immortality rather suggests it must be a vital part of our essence. It is at least defensible to suppose that such an awareness exists because we all know that we do survive.

There are three main bodies of evidence that those who explore survival point towards. These are: mediums who claim contact with the dead, memories of an existence before the present life and stories of those brought back from the brink of death to live and tell what happened. We will look at progress in each area during 1992.

Although today we associate mediums with stage performers like the late Doris Stokes, the gregarious Doris Collins and others who attract huge audiences the world over, the groundswell of belief in such a thing long predates this show-business image.

A strong religious movement known as Spiritualism, which uses mediumistic contact with the afterlife as its ministry, and scientific investigations of mediums are both a century or more old. Yet each is but a footnote to the long history of the subject which can be traced far back in time. There always have been mediums who forged a link with 'spirits', but they were not usually called by this name and were often given special attention by the society in which they lived. Even the Bible, despite Christianity's dim view of the paranormal, is full of prophets opening bridges with the next world. There seems little doubt that had Jesus lived today he would have been hailed as a great medium as well as a spiritual leader and would no doubt have utilized the technology of the age.

Nevertheless, the subject has become rather sensationalized and most scientists regard mediums as stage shows, either preying on the bereaved whilst they are in a psychologically vulnerable state, or innocent victims of their own wishful thinking, misinterpreting human abilities to read other people's emotions as the receipt of voices from the beyond.

A recent trend has been the return of famous people, sometimes to order, as part of a publicity stunt. I had a small role in this, reporting in detail on the claims of Bill Tenuto, an American psychic who says that John Lennon 'takes over' his vocal chords and offers messages. I have several tapes of what is claimed to be Lennon speaking through Tenuto and offering information about what he calls 'the White Brotherhood', a team of people trying in their own way to influence human thinking on earth from what they say is their new home in the afterlife. In this way they hope to bring about a spiritual revolution.

I have no way of judging the Tenuto/Lennon claims. I did try to get Lennon's former wife Cynthia to listen to them and comment. This was meant only as an objective assessment to help judge the merits of the evidence, not a stunt. But she was (no doubt rightly) wary of the musician's reputation being open to abuse and preferred to opt out. Even so I think it was right to report this information for others to judge and do personally believe the medium is sincere, whatever the interpretation we place upon his story.

However, press attention for this during 1992 offended some mediums.

They were upset because there had been other more forced attempts, the most notorious of which was the British tabloid the *Sun* seeking to establish mediumistic contact with recently deceased rival newspaper proprietor Robert Maxwell, resulting in a story that helped boost sales of what would only weeks before have been a competing media source.

Marion Dampier Jeans attacked this trend in *Psychic News* (22 February) arguing as a medium herself that it created the impression that contact with famous people virtually on tap was possible. She claims this is false, adding that 'I cannot make contact with any spirit being I choose. They have to make contact with me ... Why on earth would any spirit being suddenly appear to a total stranger – whom they had never known and have nothing in common with ...?' Her genuine concerns are appreciated by many of her colleagues; although Mrs P. Oliver wrote from Somerset to say that famous people do drop in at her sittings, including latterly Robert Maxwell. She reports that this is simply because they want to talk and seek out a suitable channel.

In May medium Bill Landis reported on his series of 'demonstrations', as public performances are often called, in Virginia and Kentucky, USA. He had with him Coral Polge, an artist who draws sketches of the spirits she tunes into rather than relay auditory messages. During one of these sessions a voice intruded, telling Bill 'Lee is here'. His sitter immediately began to cry. Landis then recognised that the spirit contact was musician and performer Liberace, who conveyed information about a named person and a memento that the sitter had lost but over which she was not to worry. Later the woman admitted to the medium that she had known the pianist when he was alive. Indeed they had been friends since their teenage years.

Coral Polge meanwhile had a great success in drawing to order, something she is not fond of doing. A man wanted her to depict a friend whom he had known many years before so that he could show the person's image to his wife. He had never possessed a photograph of the man. Coral found this remarkably easy, commenting that she felt the sitter was probably a better medium than either she or Bill Landis! But when the figure appeared and she began to sketch the result seemed odd. He was like a punk rocker, which did not fit the era she expected to be representing. But the sitter was none the less enthralled. 'That's Charlie,' he announced. The man had, in fact, been an American Indian who had died young and thus had the more modern appearance that Coral had depicted.

One of the best known and respected mediums is Matthew Manning, who came to prominence in 1971 when still a teenager. He then began to produce art work in the style of famous dead painters such as Picasso and Dürer which were magnificent in detail and seemed, for many commentators, to come from the surviving spirits of these people. Manning was, however, unusually objective and matter-of-fact about his work and went on to shun public performances and fame. Although he wrote a couple of books in the early years, he has concentrated on using his abilities for healing in a manner which has won him many admirers.

In February 1992 Dr Vernon Harrison assessed Manning's productive work in a lecture to the Society for Psychical Research in London. One of the strangest aspects of this were some 603 signatures that appeared in pencil on the wall of Manning's old bedroom in a short space of time. Nobody saw them appear and they dated themselves as covering a period of several hundred years, although most were of the seventeenth, eighteenth and nineteenth centuries. Harrison, as a professional photographer, became involved because he was asked to film all the signatures when Manning's father decided that after twenty years he now wanted to redecorate the wall. Harrison was to retain a permanent record. As for the works of art, these were considered highly impressive, especially as Manning had no training and displayed no normal proficiency in the field. His ink drawings in particular are extraordinarily vivid.

Harrison concluded that both hoax and cryptomnesia (remembering information stored in the mind but consciously forgotten) do not work. He prefers the idea that these reproductions are what he termed a 'human telex', a contact with surviving parts of the post-mortem personality as opposed to actual work produced by a surviving spirit itself.

Whatever the rights or wrongs of initiating contact with famous people, it happened again on a Spanish radio station late in the year. *Psychic News* reported (19 December) that one of the century's top scientists, Sir Oliver Lodge, had returned fifty years after his death and given an interview via direct voice medium Ray Smith from Gibraltar. He claimed to be still working on his physics research and spoke of sub-atomic particles, something that was in its infancy when he died. He claimed that 'when you die it is only those protons and electrons [in your body] that change state ... Men of science know that matter can neither be created nor destroyed. The subatomic particles that are the real you continue on their infinite journey.' Lodge further claimed that he had recently helped one scientist carry out work in quantum physics for which a Nobel prize was awarded, a story unlikely to go down well with the traditionalists at *Nature* or *Scientific American*.

Other lifetimes

The idea of past lives has become something of a joke; part of the New Age California set where everyone was a princess in Ancient Atlantis. In fact it began in the 1950s when a woman accidentally 'regressed' to an Irish personality called 'Bridey Murphy' during some hypnosis therapy. Much about her life was recovered and turned into a best-selling book and hit movie (*The Search for Bridey Murphy*). The theory was that Murphy must have been a real person whose body was once inhabited by the spirit of her modern protégé. Hundreds of millions of people around the world, in fact most religions other than Christianity, do adhere to the belief that we do not live just one life but several. We return to earth regularly after a suitable 'rest' in the afterlife. Quite a number of spirit messages received via mediums also support this concept, although a few do not.

However, the problem with the Bridey Murphy case was that, whilst no conscious fabrication was involved, there was evidence that the person had, as a child, regularly been in the company of an elderly relative who spoke of life in old Ireland. Information could have been absorbed. In the altered state of consciousness that is hypnosis the brain does have access to hidden memories and is also very skilled at fantasy, as we saw from research into alien abduction claims today. Therefore, it is conceivable that in the Murphy case, and by inference most or all of the others, the past life that emerges is a fiction unwittingly invented by the brain which is using information in the subconscious but which subjects are unaware that they possess. The debate has raged ever since, with many experiments conducted. But it is almost never possible to establish anything for certain.

I worked with therapist Joe Keeton to regress a sceptical young woman over several months. The tapes depict her life as Jill Leadenoak, a pig farmer's daughter. We could get almost no information from her as she communicated in a strong accent (which greatly embarrassed the non-hypnotised woman when she first heard it played back). She told us her very mundane story, gave the names of her pigs, but could not identify her village or give the year. But she did describe in gruesome detail how the local brew was matured by dangling dead rats inside the concoction so as to give it body. Although I certainly did not know this, it turns out to be historically accurate for the period around the Middle Ages that we seem to have been delving into. We also traced the accent to Herefordshire, a location the woman that we were working with had no connections with at all (in this life anyhow!). But we got little further.

I also volunteered myself under the guidance of nurse Mary Cherrit and can attest to the strangeness of seeing images enter your mind apparently from nowhere. But it is impossible to judge whether these are fantasies or memories. I described a life in some detail of a woman whose husband walked out on her in Bristol in the eighteenth century and who was left to fend for herself in a wood at Alvington (called by the old name, Alferington), cooking stew for a passing stage coach route – a sort of prototype motorway service cafe! Obviously I have no way of knowing if I built all this up out of fragments of information once seen but long forgotten. However, I do know that I have never been there and did not consciously know that it even exists, but yet Alvington is indeed a real village in the Forest of Dean exactly where I said it was under hypnosis. So at the very least this method uncorks some fascinating hidden talents at creativity and acting.

Magician and psychic researcher Loyd Auerbach reviewed the evidence in *Fate* (December 1992) and noted that for some, past-life regression is an escape mechanism from modern humdrum lives. But that clearly is not always true. Jill Leadenoak's was a far more dull and boring existence, if indeed the pig-farming girl ever existed, than the active, media lifestyle lived by the woman who 'became' her in my experiment.

Because of the pitfalls and despite the fascination, Auerbach has concluded that 'supposed evidence brought in by past life regression [is] not good evidence for reincarnation.' Whilst it is true that there are increasing uses of 'past lives' as therapy this is not the same thing as past lives being accepted as fact. In my own case, perhaps I experienced being deserted by my husband in a past life out of a fear of being left alone in this one. By psychologically acting out the fantasy I may feel better about that idea and thus be helped.

Similarly, in real past-life therapy work, psychologists have reported working with victims of severe phobias and finding that by 'reliving' a past life under hypnosis some event occurs that seems to trigger that phobia and this can help overcome it in conscious life. Thus, if a person is afraid of the dark and relives a past life in which they are locked in a cellar for days without food and light, then this act may at least partially alleviate their fear. But it does not prove that they really were once another person who actually had been locked in a cellar and from that seed the phobia had festered for centuries.

Auerbach reports that it may not matter whether you believe or disbelieve. If it helps then it is worthwhile. He notes that we are left with an either/or situation. If a person is regressed and becomes a pirate, but comments that this is no surprise because he has always been interested in pirates, is that because the love of pirates fuelled the hypnotized imagination or because he really was once a pirate and has retained memories of those days somewhere deep in his subconscious mind?

There are cases of spontaneous past-life memories. Indeed a growth area of paranormal research is uncovering these from children aged between about four and eight years. Almost one in five such children appear to claim them. After age eight they quickly seem to fade. However, many parents are afraid to ask their children if they recall a life before birth.

Coming back from death

In today's world of medical miracles something very strange is happening. We have developed techniques where we can snatch people back from the very threshold of death and revive those who even ten or twenty years ago would have been irretrievably gone. This startling scientific reality has produced a side effect which is so remarkable that for many researchers it offers the best hope there is of proving survival of what we might term a soul or at least some non-bodily component that remains after death.

The reason is that people are coming back, seemingly in increasing numbers, with tales of what happened after they thought their life was ended. Contrary to expectation, in a few cases (estimates suggest about one in fifty victims who come close to death) the person does not simply report lapsing into unconsciousness; instead they have an experience so consistent that few doubt it is a real account of something that happened. All they do doubt is how we should interpret what that something is.

Cases of the so-called NDE (near death experience) have only been systematically collected since about 1975 but there are historical reports showing that it did occasionally happen even thousands of years ago. Typically, the stories come from someone in an accident, or on an operating table, close to the point of no return where brain activity ceases for ever and death is irreversible.

A simple story that I investigated illustrates the point. A boy was born with a heart deformity because of a serious illness that his mother had contracted when she was pregnant. At five he was considered old enough to have surgery to put in a plastic valve to save his life. This was never discussed with him as the doctors considered him too young to understand. But the first thing he said on coming round after the dangerous, lengthy operation was 'Mummy, why wouldn't the doctors talk to me when I was floating by the ceiling?' He then described drifting out of his body, free of all pain, watching the surgery and seeing the valve they put into his body. Having no concept that this was impossible, he tried to chat merrily to the team fighting to save him and was only really perturbed because they ignored him!

I verified this story with medical staff involved at the Merseyside hospital who confirmed that he had described the valve even though he never saw it prior to the operation. Of some possible relevance is that his mother was a firm believer in reincarnation. Whilst that might seem like an instantly suspicious feature, it might simply indicate that, unlike other children, this boy felt no inhibitions about describing what took place. In such a case with a disbelieving set of parents the idea that this was 'just imagination' or even 'too frightening to talk about' may have prevented any spontaneous description of events.

As we are pushing back the frontiers even further and patients are being revived much later, after life was, according to all normal signs, quite extinguished, deeper-level NDEs are emerging. The out-of-body state only seems to be the first step, reported in up to one in ten cases. It is usually followed by the person being pulled along a tunnel towards a bright light. People use their own phrases but are clearly describing the same experience. I have heard this called 'sucked into a giant vacuum cleaner' and 'like looking into a telescope and being pulled into the tube'.

There are other factors that are less often reported, notably a sense that dead relatives are present giving you the choice to either stay or return. Everyone who has returned to tell the tale says they chose to do so. I know of no case where the decision was made to stay and yet they still came back. Generally the feeling of these witnesses is that if they pass a barrier and enter the light at the end of the tunnel there will be no way back. But when they do decide not to remain they 'whip' back – 'like being on the end of a giant rubber band' one witness told me – and are instantly within their bodies experiencing pain once more.

In May a 61-year-old man from Connecticut gave a graphic account of how he watched doctors battle with his exposed heart to try to save him from death. He knew he was at the point of death and did not care. In this state he had all the above experiences but also saw a shadowy vision of the grim reaper. Some kind of allegorical image like that occurs in only a few cases and may be one of the more serious negative factors of the phenomenon. For we would presumably prefer to regard that as an hallucination or fantasy. But, if it is, why not all the NDE account?

The Connecticut man met several of his dead relatives but was told his time was not yet up. He also saw a woman he had once known who had died young from a brain tumour. She asked him to tell her parents not to cry when he returned. But, as he succinctly reported, 'how can you tell someone that while you were dead you met their daughter?'

Dr Melvin Morse, a doctor from Seattle, published his work

with dying children (*Closer to the Light*, Bantam) in 1992. He relates many detailed accounts of near death experiences, made by those who certainly had no indoctrination or expectation about life after death. One young boy who eventually died from meningitis told Morse, after an NDE during a near miss where his heart stopped beating for three minutes, that he went to a beautiful place with radiant light and saw the doctors revive him. Before he finally succumbed he informed Morse that 'I am not afraid to go back to that place.'

Indeed, in almost every single case the NDE banishes fear of death utterly and permanently. That is its most amazing feature. As these are not stories of what happens after death, merely what happens near to it, this is not justifiable. But there is no way to tell that to those who have had such an experience. They simply profess to know that death is neither painful nor frightening. In fact they often call it 'wonderful'.

The most common arguments against accepting any reality from the NDE is the medical theory that it results from some natural cause. Hallucinations triggered by anaesthetics or administered drugs was once a favourite, until it was conclusively shown that the NDEs reported in accidents or emergency surgery where no drugs are given match the other cases too closely. Clearly, therefore, drugs are not the cause.

A replacement theory suggested the visions are a consequence of anoxia (lack of oxygen to the brain) and not dissimilar to the dissociative state reported by some mountaineers at heights where the oxygen content of the atmosphere is very thin. However, surgeon Dr Michael Sabom has a case where blood gases were measured at the point of NDE, and so it seems not to matter whether there is or is not oxygen flow to the brain, or whether there are or are not other indications of anoxia.

However, in 1992 Dr Susan Blackmore, from the department of psychology at the University of Western England, came up with a more sophisticated rationalist theory that has been subjected to much debate. There can be no disputing that Dr Blackmore, whilst sceptical, is an accredited parapsychologist. She has done extensive work in paranormal areas such as the out-of-body state, written definitive books and earned great respect from both sides of the parapsychological divide. That is something very few scientists can claim. Dr Blackmore wrote extensively about her 'dying brain' theory in sources such as

Wild Places (5), *PSI Researcher* (Summer 1992) and a lecture to the Society for Psychical Research on 10 December, later summarised in *Psychic News* (26 December). She has also announced a book expanding the concept for summer 1993 *Dying to Live*, Grafton).

The first important point she makes is that NDEs do not only occur when the person is, literally, near death. Some of the symptoms have been reliably reported from someone who merely feared that they were dying, or were under intense stress, but were physically in no danger. She cites a mountaineer falling hundreds of feet into soft snow and surviving relatively unscathed. It may, of course, be possible that these people were nearly 'frightened to death', and expectation of imminent death may be the critical factor, but it certainly is a point against the strict definition of an NDE occurring during the final moments of life from which medicine then snatches the patient back. She then attempts to show that the sceptics' view that they are meaningless hallucinations, as well as the parapsychology approach that they are evidence for post-death survival, are both unacceptable.

She proposes that endorphins, natural chemicals that deaden pain when a body is subjected to physical trauma, may induce some of the NDE symptoms. She also believes that the cells in the optic neurone network will be exhausting their oxygen and therefore fire randomly. As the exhaustion nears completion this would increase in speed. She has simulated this by computer and found that, because there are more cells in the centre than at the periphery of vision, the result is optically similar to a bright light at the centre of darkness along which you seem to be pulled.

As for the feeling of reality that the experience undeniably has, she believes this occurs simply because the brain seizes on the retinal firing as the only element of stability in a rapidly deteriorating set of order and thus interprets this as real. We therefore believe in the NDE as real because our dying brain has told us to. The brain may even create a model of the self (as an out-of-body vision of one's own image) in order to help preserve a feeling of self-existence when all other indicators of this are rapidly crumbling. Because the NDE victim has experienced life at the raw edge of existence, where their brain almost dissolved into nothingness and ego vanished, the person comes back to reality greatly changed, having a very different view of the world because of the comparison with this selfless state from which they have returned.

The theory holds together well, seeming to account for much of the NDE. But I do wonder if a brain snatched back from this near dissolution would really cherish that experience and look forward to a return, relegating life to a lesser importance and almost perceiving death as the better place to be. Surely, if Dr Blackmore's theory is correct, then the firmness and preciousness of life would be clung to with greater intensity and the NDE patient would be terrified of the prospect of heading back one day into that maelstrom of ego-less uncertainty where 'you' vanish? This very definitely is not what NDE witnesses report.

Dr Blackmore's rationalist views reaffirm, she says, that there is no soul and that survival stories are simply told to ourselves to deny our own extinction. Not surprisingly this inspired much debate from other parapsychologists. Indeed much of *PSI Researcher* (Autumn 1992) was devoted to this ongoing critique and Dr Blackmore's considered replies to it. This, for me, is what real paranormal research is all about.

John Smythies, from the Institute of Neurology at the National Hospital in London, was one of the first to challenge her thesis. He calls her ideas 'ingenious' but is not persuaded by them. He argued against many of her claims about the way the optical process works and notes that, whilst a more complex reductionist theory might still be found, hers does not succeed. He does, however, have some support for the arguments against the NDE being a survival experience. He notes that victims who suffer an optical lobectomy (i.e. having that part of their brain destroyed) not only become blind but lose any awareness of what sight is. Similar problems arise when they lose parts that control the sense of body image. Thus, he feels, any disembodied mind could not exist in an afterlife and have the kind of concept of body, self or visions that NDE victims and mediums suggest. On the other hand, Smythies does point out that outside space and time we have no way of knowing what a different perception might be like. It may be 'far more splendid than any spatial world.'

Blackmore effectively responded to his charges but noted ultimately that they had a different interpretation of what neuroscience (the study of the brain) was doing to the concept of self. He, as a neurologist, believed this remained intact, she, as a psychologist, felt its recent progress had dispensed with the need to have any self 'as being something that acts, chooses and decides ... I think the coming years in this exciting science will force us to overthrow some of our most cherished notions about the power of our conscious selves and accept our basic biological nature.'

David Fontana, like Dr Blackmore a psychologist, also found her work valuable but notes more important problems, particularly that the tunnel imagery seems to occur in limited cases only (he cited several studies averaging out at under one in three NDE victims). As such her optical firing theory has to contend with the fact that two-thirds of the NDE data does not have reports of one of its key tenets.

Sue Blackmore thinks this crucial, but that it supports her theory. She noted studies that imply that the tunnel image is more common in patients who come closest to medical death as opposed to those who fear they might die but are in less physical danger. Whilst, as I noted earlier, this makes sense if, in fact, the tunnel is a later-stage NDE phenomenon and thus only occurs if you get very close to the point of no return, Blackmore sees it very differently. She points out that the tunnel could only emerge from the firing of optical neurones in the brain cortex if that is severely impaired as death approaches. In cases where there is no serious physical trauma it ought not to happen. You pay your money and take your choice. But this can be tested.

However, Fontana also wonders why, if the self-image and ego are breaking up, those who experience deep NDE report the most control, for example being given a choice, arguing that their family needs them, talking to dead relatives, and so on? This seems less like a mind on the point of dissolution than one that is very much alive and kicking.

Dr Blackmore suggests that because the internally generated imagery has no rival input it takes on a vividness and realism that it might not have otherwise and that witness descriptions of the choices faced are, she feels, 'extremely equivocal ... they give the impression they are struggling to put into words events that don't fit our usual ideas of a self who makes choices.'

Possibly one of the most critical points Dr Blackmore makes is that there is no objective verification that she could trace proving that in the NDE state the witness has seen something they could not have seen without being 'out of the body'. In fact there are some claims that this does happen. I have myself investigated two cases (one of which is that of the young boy with the heart valve, the other a man who had an allergic reaction to Heparin and nearly died.) In both of these medical staff did confirm to me that the patients described things they were not in any position to see from their location prone on the bed and, in the nursing staff's view, deeply unconscious. There are many similar cases the world over.

However, Dr Blackmore investigated two of the most important. In one a woman who had been blind from birth allegedly had visual experiences during an NDE. When she checked with the author who published the story he candidly admitted he made it up to illustrate a point, not realizing that others would take it so seriously!

The second case, usually known as the 'tennis shoe' incident, is possibly the most significant. Dr Blackmore claims she was unable to discover more than the anecdotal account. However, researchers from the Society of Psychical Research have since enlightened her and interviews with the participants were filmed, screened and seem to verify the substance of this story. The event happened in a Seattle hospital and involved Professor Kim Clark-Sharp who was treating a 50-year-old woman when she went into full cardiac arrest. There was no heartbeat or pulse. After resuscitation the woman told her doctor that she had floated by the ceiling and was able to describe who had been in the room, what they had done and the equipment used. Professor Clark-Sharp stated that this proved accurate.

However, the most curious thing was the woman's insistence that she had been distracted by floating outside the room and seeing a tennis shoe on the third-floor ledge of the hospital. How had it got there? The doctor was surprised. There was clearly no shoe visible from the window of the room. But the patient insisted. Here was a real chance to test the authenticity of the woman's astonishing story, so Professor Clark-Sharp bravely ventured out and, sure enough, found a trainer had somehow been deposited out of sight round the corner. She brought it back, hid it from the woman and asked her to describe it. She did so correctly, giving the colour as blue.

The apparent verification of this story may affect Dr

Blackmore's verdict since she has shown her willingness to base theories on facts and results, as indeed is how it should be.

Undoubtedly, Sue Blackmore's theory is one of the most pertinent sceptical viewpoints put forward in some time and deserves attention and discussion. But she does quite rightly note that 'we have barely begun' debating the options and that, although she is convinced 'that we will ultimately succeed in explaining all the elements of the NDE in terms of processes in the dying (or threatened) brain' that 'the nice thing is that I cannot say who is right and who is wrong – only time will tell.' If only more critics of the paranormal were as thorough, determined, perceptive and honest as Sue Blackmore.

UFOs

This was a very busy year for UFO activity. Generally the number of sightings showed an upturn for the first time since the late 1970s and UFO organisations the world over were reporting a boom in membership. MUFON (Mutual UFO Network) in the USA were printing over 4000 copies of its monthly magazine and BUFORA (British UFO Research Association) had a higher number in its network than it had had for more than a decade.

The year itself saw some very different events. For example, the field lost one of its great pioneers, French science writer Aimé Michel, who died just after Christmas. His work had uncovered some of the classic cases of the 1950s and his books were perhaps the first ever written that looked at the subject with a scientific eye. At the other extreme a museum was opened in Roswell, New Mexico, to mark the location of an infamous incident in July 1947 when, so many UFO researchers allege, an alien aircraft exploded in mid air and crashed into the desert. It was an event, they contend, that changed world history.

There is no disputing that something did come down. Even the sceptics accept that. Stories have circulated for years about the debris collected from rancher Mac Brazel's land, ferried back to Roswell Air Force base and then on (it is said) to Wright Patterson in Dayton, Ohio. The flimsy material with allegedly unusual tensile strength that could not be dented by a sledgehammer hardly sounds like the fabric of an alien spacecraft, but that is what a preliminary press release implied. However, this was quickly replaced by another that announced it was, in fact, just a weather balloon and remains of one of these (said to be the object collected) were shown to the cameras. However, all the eyewitnesses denied this, including the base officer who collected it painstakingly from the desert floor. Until his dying day he insisted that he did not know what the object was that fell outside Roswell, but it was no weather balloon. That had just been a cover story to put the media off whilst they flew the debris to Wright Patterson for detailed study.

Half a century later the debate still rages and a Hollywood movie is being planned that will tell a version of the tale. The sceptics say it was just a balloon. Many leaders of the American UFO community say it was an unknown craft from beyond the earth. However, claims that alien bodies were recovered from the wreckage have not been substantiated and are not endorsed by some researchers who have spent years chasing evidence.

In Chicago in February 1992 a seminar was held to debate new evidence that had arisen following an *Unsolved Mysteries* television dramatization during September 1989. This purported to be clear evidence from an eyewitness who saw the dead bodies that were found at the site. Researchers taking opposing views presented their case and the arguments were published in a special booklet by the Center for UFO Studies. By the end of 1992 the majority feeling amongst most knowledgable researchers was that the new evidence had been found wanting and that the case for the recovery of alien bodies at Roswell was as shaky as before.

Stalwart UFOlogist John Keel, a New York journalist, spoke his mind at a lecture in Sheffield in August. He offered his own radical interpretation of the case, accepting that a strange object had come down but arguing that it was a Japanese balloon bomb!

Japan launched hundreds of explosive devices tethered to high altitude balloons in a war of attrition against the USA during World War II. Many of these never made it across the treacherous Pacific skies but a few did and some damage and casualties are known to have been caused by these US mainland bombings. Even well after the war balloon bomb debris was still being found in remote parts of the western USA.

Keel proposes that the Roswell object might have been a rogue flight possibly launched by a diehard Japanese commander refusing to accept defeat. Certainly the explosion heard by rancher Brazel, the way the debris was scattered about and the form of the remains are more consistent with an unfamiliar type of balloon than they are with a structured machine that navigated space. In addition the witnesses did mention 'hieroglyphics' or oriental writing that was found on the side of the debris picked up at the site, and Keel further noted that the Japanese had techniques for making incredibly strong but very light and paper-like material for such balloon flights. Keel succinctly argued that the evidence fitted together very well and that it is likely that the Roswell staff might not have recognized the object for what it was; but that when defence staff did they would inevitably have hidden the truth to prevent a diplomatic incident.

However, William Moore from California, one of the first researchers probing into the Roswell case, eloquently tried to defend the position, from his work with dozens of witnesses, that the material was too strange to come from a balloon and was a UFO in the traditional sense.

Either way the museum in Roswell will offer visitors the opportunity to see some of this story, but unfortunately not any of the debris – as that was all long since confiscated by the military!

This belief in a cover-up of information, hard evidence and (to some) even UFO wreckage and dead bodies of aliens is very strong in the USA. It is rather more frowned upon elsewhere; although even in sceptical nations such as Britain there is undeniable evidence that some things are being obscured if national security demands it and, regardless of their public stance on UFOs, collation of data about the subject continues within the Ministry of Defence. However, I have found that the MoD are generally helpful and whenever they can do so tend to channel witnesses to BUFORA so that their sightings can be investigated; they also supply us with copies of any reports they have received via their sources which might possibly correlate with any such event. This new open attitude is greatly appreciated by myself and the BUFORA investigations team that I coordinate.

None the less, in the USA, Operation Right to Know was launched on 28 March 1992 by a small team of Americans who decided to try to pressure the authorities into revelations. They staged a demonstration outside the White House carrying banners stating 'end the UFO cover up' and chanting 'Yo! Yo! UFO! The people have a right to know!' But it seems that the good-natured affair had most impact on a group of Japanese tourists who handed round cameras so that they could be filmed in the company of this extraordinary testament to democracy.

Operation Right to Know are looking to expand their activities and are keen to recruit help from willing demonstration organizers (see address on page 187).

In France, there has been a rather more open policy for some time. In 1974 the then Minister of Defence, Robert Galley discussed UFOs freely on national radio and admitted there were cases that baffled his government, including instances where French Air Force jets had been vectored on to targets that were tracked by radar.

As a result of this astonishing, but outside France little reported, speech, a team of scientists was set up at the space centre in Toulouse and began to investigate landing cases in some depth. Many years later it has undergone changes but still exists, although not being quite as forthcoming about the release of its reports as it was in the heyday of the late 1970s aand early 1980s. Then some invaluable case histories on unexplained sightings were put together.

However, French UFO journal *OVNI* (August 1992) published a new interview with Galley in which he talked about how his views have changed since 1974. He takes a very objective line about UFOs, aware that they can contribute to scientific knowledge but not jumping to conclusions about their being spacecraft. Asked about the wave of triangular UFOs seen in Belgium during 1989, 1990 and 1991 which, despite suspicions to the contrary, the Americans have denied were their stealth aircraft technology being test-flown, Galley felt that it was possible they were secret terrestrial technology or aircraft. He told of an incident where an American plane from a base in Germany flew over Pierrelatte, a location where the French have a plant to enrich uranium. Galley explained that the film taken by the jet was picked up by a high-level colonel and, although they later found out about this, claimed 'the Americans had not informed us'. Meanwhile, in Scotland a rather different battle was afoot. For some years the Scottish group SPI (Strange Phenomena Investigations) and Ron Halliday and Malcolm Robinson in particular had been attempting to persuade Livingston new town development corporation to commemorate a classic UFO event on their forest parkland.

The incident happened in November 1979 when a forestry worker was attacked by two objects from a landed disc and rendered unconscious. Police treated it as a possible assault and even cordoned off the area. Steuart Campbell produced an excellent special report that was published by BUFORA, and the story itself seems genuine enough.

Robinson, Halliday and SPI wanted the corporation to mark the site in Dechmont Law with a plaque and showed remarkable perseverance in pushing for what they anticipated would be a 'world's first'. But they were up against what to me looks like a fairly cynical attitude. Eventually, the corporation accepted the idea but came up with what I feel was a wishy-washy inscription. Effectively it was a plug for UFO debunker Arthur C. Clarke, noting that he had happened to mention the incident in a book some time afterwards (hardly an earthshaking moment); as far as I know he had had no part in the months of investigation which painstakingly established the importance of this case. Indeed, Clarke has very specific views about UFOs. He does not believe in them.

Consequently SPI, I felt quite correctly, proposed that the corporation come up with some better wording to stand as monument at this spot. Not only did the corporation refuse but they went ahead and mounted the plaque without informing the witness (whose name was not even given second billing in the wording to Arthur C. Clarke!) and without telling the UFOlogists who had pushed for the idea. Despite this treatment, Malcolm Robinson showed generous forgiveness and went out of his way to help promote the existence of the plaque, which the corporation had not seemed keen to do. Various national press stories followed, which promoted Livingston new town to good effect, but a spokesman for the corporation was quick to stress that Robinson and Halliday were incorrect to suggest the plaque was a world's first, because it 'merely quotes Arthur C. Clarke's book ... the corporation is not acknowledging that any such sighting took place' (*Lothian Courier*, 17 January). They elaborated (*Scotsman*, same date) that they had deliberately only mentioned sceptic Clarke because 'as an official body (we) do not want to endorse the encounter.' One might then justifiably wonder why they bothered to put up the plaque in the first place?

Whatever the case, SPI were determined not to let the moment pass and set up their own opening ceremony in the park on 14 May. The Glasgow rock band CE IV (a CE IV being an incident like that which the forester experienced) set up their stage gear, including a life-sized model alien, and they and the

UFOlogists posed for the cameras, expressing pride at this Scottish achievement which the development corporation themselves seemed nearly embarrassed by.

Sadly, just as some feel that a witness might have been 'abducted' in some cases, the plaque itself was subjected to mysterious forces when it vanished from its cairn during October. Determined to do something rather better as a replacement Ron Halliday launched a campaign later that month to raise funds and come up with a design for a more permanent monument, perhaps a statue. He wants to reflect the location where this incident took place to best advantage. Of course, it remains to be seen if the development corporation will agree to that and be a little more positive in any accompanying inscription. In any case, as events were to prove, the UFOs themselves had the last laugh in Scotland!

Sightings of the year

1992 began and ended with fun and games in Scotland, which was undoubtedly the tourist hot spot for would be UFO spotters.

On 3 January a brilliant object flashed across the Shetland Islands. Bemused crofters on this remote place saw the object as a fiery red disc looking 'like a world globe'. In the closest approach it was seen at ground level and projected what looked like an electric tube to the earth, then climbed into the sky, falling apart and growing dimmer. The light from the landed object had illuminated one farmhouse at Sand, as attested by the crofter's sister and his wife. Astronomers suggested it might have been an 'electric meteor' but the description barely matches that.

After the fuss over the Livingston UFO plaque the *Scotsman* carried an article (26 September) entitled 'Where on earth did the Martians go?' which, ironically, cited some figures from me that suggested UFO sightings were diminishing. That might have been true prior to 1992 but the year was already reversing the trend. The figures I had compiled seem artificially low because investigators today tend not to follow up misidentifications. As over 90 per cent of all sightings are cases of mistaken identity, removing most of these from statistics makes it seem as if all the UFOs have gone away.

This article was ironic because four weeks later my book *UFOs and How to See Them* was released showing that Scotland was a strong focal point for UFO activity in Britain. The Scottish media took to this quickly and I made several appearances on television and radio and in the national press endorsing this opinion. As I spoke of this status the Livingston plaque was hijacked and, it seems, the UFOs paid attention because Scotland was immediately hit by an unprecedented wave of sightings.

There were two areas of intense activity between October and December which generated over a hundred sightings between them. One was the village of Muchalls near Aberdeen where red and white cylinders were flying about the sky on a regular basis. The other was in the Hallglen and Bonnybridge area of Lothian where witnesses were getting quite concerned about the level of light-in-the-sky reports. Undoubtedly some of the sightings were Venus (very bright in the early evening sky late in the year) and meteors, a whole series of which produced bright sky spectaculars during December. Others were less easy to account for.

A councillor in the Bonnybridge area actually called in UFOlogists to help calm down the population and both Malcolm Robinson and Ron Halliday responded. Indeed Halliday set up a hotline for callers to report events and obtain solace and this was very busy in the lead-up to Christmas.

Green fireballs have been common in the Lothian skies, although there was an interesting report from the moors near Hallglen where a big blue light landed on the road in front of some startled walkers and was followed by a rattling noise as if a door fell open, then a brilliant flash as if their photographs were being taken. Perhaps the beauties of the Scottish countryside were attracting the tourist industry from an unexpected source!

In the USA an increasingly common UFO type, the triangle or boomerang, was reported in the Williamsport, Pennsylvania area on the evening of 5 February. Dozens of people independently described the low rumbling noise ('like a freight train' or 'Niagara falls' were two descriptions of this sound) which moved at exceptionally slow speed across the sky. The witnesses could walk underneath what was a huge object and keep pace with it. It comprised many lights on a wide 'V' formation that was dark and hard to spot against the sky.

Dr Sam Greco, an expert in propulsion, checked this out for PASU (the Pennsylvania Association for the study of unexplained phenomena) and MUFON. The aviation authorities said no flight plans had been filed and his first-class study in the town reached no conclusions, but I have to say that there are marked similarities between this incident and several that have occurred in Britain since 1987.

These have been found to be military exercises involving heavy tanker aircraft and smaller jets flying in close formation. The aim is to practice refuelling in mid air for long-range bombing missions. Because the flights often originate miles from where they line up and are observed, and as the military (normally the US Air Force) seem reluctant to advertise what they are doing, both local airports and police, whom media and witnesses consult, say they are unaware of any air traffic. They insist that nothing was flying, which may well be locally true, and the case acquires legendary proportions.

In fact, in the cases I have looked at, there are many aircraft passing by very high up (possibly eight miles or more). They are spread over a large area but the human mind assumes that these are part of one big object, not separate aircraft flying together. An odd-looking shape is thus filled in between the lights, partly by imagination and from dimly perceived outlines of the real aircraft. Several heavy planes flying high in the sky would produce the rumbling sounds described in Pennsylvania. The extremely slow speed is just an illusion caused by the fact that the mind assumes it is seeing a relatively small object fairly low down, and thus moving with peculiar stealth. In fact it is watching a far larger group of objects a lot higher in the sky which are moving at their normal speed. However, because of their unexpected distance from the witness, they seem to someone on the ground to move very slowly.

It is rather less easy to find a solution for the sightings on 27 June at Raeford, North Carolina. Here a nurse's assistant and her mother heard a noise like a roaring train from their mobile home which shook violently in response. Outside they saw an object on the ground with a curved row of windows glowing orange. Their outside light had failed prior to the arrival of this object, as had that of their neighbour's home. They went out for a better look but the object suddenly vanished and their outside light came back on again. Several others on distant properties then went off as if the object was flying away and blanking these out. An investigation by MUFON investigators Rick Heldreth and Wayne Laporte was mounted and examined a swirled grass area which was flattened and discoloured as if an object had landed there. The local sheriff's office also investigated and the witnesses were visited by a man claiming to be from the US military but asking odd questions. This seems to have been what UFOlogists call a 'man in black' visitation.

On 8 August an interesting investigation was conducted by BUFORA researchers Ken Phillips and Judith Jafaar. A family were driving to a shopping centre in Milton Keynes when they suddenly entered a peculiar aura. Although it was a busy Saturday morning they all stopped laughing and talking, 'went in on themselves', traffic vanished, sounds stopped and they encountered a sudden oval bank of thick fog. They ran into this, then out the other side to discover that they had moved from Hockliffe in Bedfordshire to further down the road and nearer to their destination. This was not a 'time lapse' as such, more a sort of teleportation or 'space lapse' effect. It involves no typical UFO but clearly seems unusual in some way. In the past similar situations have been explored under hypnosis and an 'alien abduction' memory emerged. This has not been attempted here, although the witnesses report that when they got out of their car they felt very strange. They had lost all sense of coordination and missed the door handle when they tried to grab it. This is also an effect reported in other close encounter cases and may be connected with the altered state of consciousness from which they are emerging. They felt 'out of synch', confused about time, and both adults found strange red patches on their bodies that faded after a few days. So peculiar was the sensation of 'not being right' that one of the witnesses felt they might have had a car crash and died. She went to her mother later that morning to assure herself they were 'still alive'.

UFO Research Australia report an unusual incident in the early afternoon of 14 September involving Australian Airlines flight 405 on its way to Hobart in Tasmania. Ten minutes out and passing at 18,000 feet over Miena a passenger saw a black cigar-shaped object that was hovering in the sky. The aircraft flew past and the UFO was masked by hills west of Derwent. Although the reporting witness is sure others saw it, the crew were traced and did not. The local weather bureau suggested an unusual cloud formation but were unable to verify this idea from their records.

The case seems important because it is extremely similar to several others that have been reported to UFO groups recently, including one from an Aeroflot plane over Russia and another from a jet circling above Los Angeles. A pilot of a private jet from Norfolk also took a photograph of a dark black cylinder as he was flying above the Nevada desert. Consequently this does appear to be a novel type of UFO that for some reason is now being persistently seen by passengers in aircraft. At times the aircraft's own shadow can be projected on to cloud and seems peculiar to passengers who are not frequent travellers. But the details of these cases under review seem to rule out that option.

The sceptics' approach to UFOs

As you can see, UFOlogists themselves are careful and quite often solve cases. Sometimes that can take a very long time to achieve.

In January 1973 building surveyor Peter Day took a piece of film lasting twenty-three seconds, depicting an orange ball of light moving slowly across the horizon on the Buckinghamshire/Oxfordshire border. Some school children at nearby Long Crendon saw the oval tinged with red fly almost overhead and a teacher travelling to the school saw it from a car at a third location. This invaluable series of witnesses plus a daylight film allowed mathematics to calculate the size and shape of the object. A detailed report can be found in *UFO Reality* (Hale, 1983), in which a colour still from the film is also included on the cover.

From the start it was known that a USAF F-111 jet crashed that morning on a flight from Upper Heyford. Peter Day offered the film to the airbase for their accident enquiry the minute he heard about this on the news, but when they discovered he had filmed it at just after 9 a.m. – over forty minutes before the aircraft crashed some thirty miles away – they expressed no interest and Day was left to assume he had filmed a UFO.

Considerable investigation followed over many years and I compiled what we knew into a special report entitled 'Fire in the Sky' (BUFORA, 1988). A Hollywood movie about UFOs was released in 1993 and adopts an identical title, but is not about the Day film.

In 'Fire in the Sky' I explained that all the years of work had led to two possibilities. Either the object filmed was an unusual atmospheric electrical effect that might have precipitated the accident to the aircraft, or the cameraman filmed, and the witnesses saw, a ball of fire lit by burning fuel from the F-111 as it struggled to correct its fault. Either way there had to be a connection, because the F-111 first developed problems at almost the exact moment the UFO sighting occurred, even though it kept in the air for some time after that. Because the crew had safely ejected using a new rocket propulsion system details of the accident enquiry were kept quiet and BUFORA had had no success getting an official report to help choose between these options.

One-time BUFORA investigator, later sceptical writer, Steuart Campbell published reports on the incident in which he claimed to have solved the case, implying that BUFORA had failed to do so. In fact his solution was one of the two taken above from 'Fire in the Sky', which the team had specifically suggested four years before. It was important that Campbell had now secured a copy of the accident report, via the Freedom of Information laws of the USA. This was very useful and shows conclusively that the F-111 developed a problem with its fuel line on take-off. Then shortly after 9 a.m., whilst in the correct position and flying in the same direction as the UFO, it ejected fuel to try to lighten the load to make an emergency landing. The fuel was ignited by the afterburner but after only a couple of minutes was switched off. This is all quite consistent with what witnesses saw.

I have talked to Peter Day and he is understandably reluctant to accept this conclusion. He points out that he heard nothing, and a jet with afterburners is very noisy, as he knew from living close to the Upper Heyford base. This is a fair point, but the F-111 was some way north of the cameraman and could have been inaudible. The schoolchildren in their yard, no doubt playing and ready to start the day, were closer but were inevitably making a lot of noise. This might conceivably have prevented the aircraft from being heard by them. It was then flying at 2000 feet, just above the cloud ceiling. So the plane itself would have been invisible, but the ejected ball of fuel, possibly trapped by a thermal layer at the cloud base, would have shone through and, via this veil of cloud, might well have looked extremely odd.

All UFO cases come down to a question of choices. That is true here. But I think the hard work expended by UFOlogists on this case, despite Steuart Campbell's unfair failure to credit them for it, did uncover all the basic facts that allow you to reach your own judgement on these events. In my view that is all that can be expected of any investigation.

Another set of events that was put under severe scrutiny during 1992 were those that hit the Wessex town of Warminster during the 1960s. Crop circle hoaxers Doug and Dave say they deliberately located circles in this area to play on the reputation of the town as a UFO Mecca in the 'Hippy' era. Now some serious doubts have arisen as to how much of the original reputation which the town acquired is justified.

The 'Warminster Thing' was seen and photographed regularly from the mid sixties onward and local journalist Arthur Shuttlewood published a series of articles in the national press and books during the next ten years which sent UFO spotters rushing to the hillsides looking for their own encounters. Local barns still sport UFO graffiti as a result of these skywatches, and, whilst it was accepted that a lot of what was seen was probably the result of military activity on Salisbury Plain, there were some puzzling encounters that preserved the reputation of this region.

In January 1992 a man sent me a copy of a letter that he had posted to the BUFORA offices in Hertfordshire. It was for the attention of vice-chairman John Spencer and made some startling revelations, directing us to a man who could provide proof of these and including some evidence to back this up. The matter was pursued and John Spencer published his conclusions in *UFO Times* (Spring 1992). The magazine used one of the best titles of the year, the very appropriate 'Warminster Wilts'.

What was being alleged? Spencer went to meet another man called Roger Hooton, as the letter directed. Here he was told that the photograph of 'the thing' which journalist Arthur Shuttlewood had first publicized across the double page centre spread of the *Daily Mirror* on 10 September 1965 was, in fact, a hoax played on him. On it much of Warminster's reputation depended. If it really was now found doubtful then much reassessment was necessary.

John Spencer's report states that he learnt that the UFO was a model made from milk-bottle tops, buttons and a cotton reel. One can see this possibility in the graphic daylight image reproduced of a disk, reputedly taken on 29 August over this Wiltshire town.

The hoax was supposedly cooked up in a pub by a group of people as a joke to catch out the owner of the local paper, on which Shuttlewood worked at the time. They had deliberately ensured that the pictures on the film either side of the negative of the UFO did not match their story. Had anyone done what all investigators are taught to do today and checked the entire set of negatives, not just the one showing the UFO, this would probably have been spotted right away. But in those days a UFO picture was considered impervious to explanation and was commonly accepted by all comers at face value. Other clues were seeded into the photograph but seemingly not spotted by investigators or media in 1965.

John Spencer is continuing to investigate the Warminster affair because it was a significant turning-point in British UFO history. There are still unanswered questions and the man who claimed to have taken the photograph has yet to be traced or to comment on these allegations. But if it was a joke, then how much, if any, of the subsequent stories about 'the thing', car stoppages, strange sounds and the like were further hoaxes in what is said to have been a chain of incidents? Either way the foundation upon which the reputation of this UFO hot spot was built must be said to have taken quite a battering.

A modern-day equivalent of Warminster in many respects is Gulf Breeze, on the north Florida coast near the naval base at Pensacola. Since 1987 countless photographs have been taken and sightings made of lighted objects in the sky. Just as at Warminster a quarter of a century ago skywatches are held almost nightly and UFO watchers flock there from all around the world.

There has been a protracted debate inside UFOlogy about the status of the numerous polaroid photographs which set the ball rolling. These were taken over many nights between November 1987 and May 1988 (but not since) by local businessman Ed Walters. He published a book on the subject (*The Gulf Breeze Sightings*, William Morrow, 1990).

The conflict of opinion is well shown by *MUFON Journal*

during 1992. In July the cover story 'Bona fide or bogus?' was by William Hyzer, a highly qualified specialist in optical instrumentation and forensic photographic analysis. His research had been commissioned by MUFON, one of the staunchest defenders of the reality of the Gulf Breeze polaroids, having supported them within the book and on countless occasions since. His conclusions seem very specific. For a number of reasons, but particularly because a shot of a UFO hovering low over a roadway did not produce a reflection in the bodywork of the car (as experiments showed that it ought to have done) it was proposed that the evidence pointed to the photographs being trick shots by way of double exposure methods.

This view was, of course, subjected to intense criticism by other investigators. In the October edition Jeff Staino, a photoanalyst with MUFON and manager of an imaging research company, reassessed the most damning evidence. He says that working with first generation prints provided by Walters, which Hyzer claims the witness denied to him, Staino had found evidence of the missing car reflection. Hyzer pointed out in reply that there is no way for anyone unfamiliar with the niceties of this subject to decide who is right if critics, like himself, have no access to the use of the original photographs to do work like his own.

Hyzer also noted that in a paper to the 1992 MUFON conference ('Photo analysis: a pictorial primer') Staino made the startling suggestion that UFOs might deliberately make themselves look like 'fakes or misidentifications' so as to deflect witnesses from the truth. This suggestion may, of course, prove to be true. But the problem with such an unusual theory is that it effectively means you can never disprove a UFO photograph. If your analysis finds features within it suggesting that it might be a hoax, then these can always be countered by alleging that the aliens made it look that way on purpose. However, irrespective of these probably insoluble arguments about the Walters photographs (which the photographer himself still insists are quite genuine) the Gulf Breeze affair has more to it. Many other people have seen and photographed things.

Dr Bruce Maccabee, an optical physicist, has been one of the leading lights in this research and in *International UFO Reporter* (January 1992) describes some of the other events in that

Florida town. These contain camcorder images taken of the orange, white and red ovals of light that drift across the sky and then wink out. In May 1992 Maccabee himself filmed one of these, which I saw a few weeks later. It was also filmed by two television cameras, one a black and white telephoto, the other a more standard colour type. All three show details of the object and the close range image appears to show a burning piece of debris falling off.

This effect has been noticed in several other sightings from the town and the theory has been proposed that some of the locals are playing jokes on skywatchers by creating sightings from flares and home-made hot-air balloons. Zan Overall outlined the idea in *International UFO Reporter* (March 1992), but it should be added that he is a long-term critic of the case and such reports have upset some American UFOlogists. He has claimed, for instance, that a model plan of an object like those on Walters' pictures was found buried under insulation in the businessman's old home. Walters' supporters argue that this must have been planted there by a sceptic out to destroy the case's credibility. Overall says he has also talked to Thomas Smith, a young man who insists that he was party to creating photographs, but this is again utterly rejected by both witnesses and many UFOlogists in the USA.

Another claim that Smith made to Overall was that he knew of plans to use home-made balloons. These were created from large plastic bags filled with hot air pumped in by way of a hairdryer or by tying lighted candles to the base. More sophisticated methods, it is suspected, might use flares attached to the bag. The hot air causes the balloon to rise and the candles or flares make it glow. It then drifts with the wind like a glowing ball of light until it goes out suddenly when the flare or candles expire. At times part of the plastic may melt or catch fire and this can drip to earth in a process that looks like a chain of debris or fall of sparks, almost as if the UFO is dispatching a mini-projectile back to earth. Certainly the video images that Maccabee screened in June 1992 could be interpreted as such a balloon.

Overall claims that the American Federal Aviation Administration are looking carefully into the possibility of widespread hoax balloon launches because of the air traffic from the Pensacola base and the risk of a disastrous mid-air collision that might accidentally result.

Interestingly, and quite independently, the *Skeptic* magazine

(May 1992) had a piece by Dave Mitchell owning up to his own balloon hoaxing. His very humorous account of his activities shows how he launched several different balloons involving black bags and much larger transparent ones during a time when there was a wave of sightings in Wales in 1977. Mitchell's claimed experiments once even alerted an air–sea rescue helicopter, and he thought very seriously about using metal to make them radar-reflective in an attempt to attract local fighter command, but rather fortunately decided against this plan.

Balloons of the home-made hot-air variety, just like those allegedly flying over Gulf Breeze, have dogged researchers in north-west England for at least ten years. Sightings in the Rossendale Valley, in particular, have involved drifting orange lights which dribble fiery debris to the ground ('like a ladder unfolding' is a common description). The local press has often reported these 'UFOs', although they have also drifted over other parts of Lancashire. The balloon theory was soon established as a front-runner by experienced investigators but was only proven in 1992 when a member of what is now the Lancashire Aerial Phenomenon Investigation Society told me about being covertly approached by the culprits who admitted to their nocturnal adventures. Indeed, it was my familiarity with this type of home-made UFO that helped me feel very suspicious about some of the lights drifting over Gulf Breeze. Of course, whether the entire mystery in these Florida skies is scuppered by this sort of solution is quite another matter.

Flying the unfriendly skies

Balloons also figured in one of the most worrying UFO stories of 1992, the revelation that the year before there had been several all too close encounters between passenger aircraft and strange objects over the skies of southern England. Whether UFOs or IFOs (identified flying objects) these events have serious repercussions for our crowded skies.

The first case had been reported in 1991. It had happened on 21 April when an Alitalia MD 80 jet from Milan to London encountered a dark missile-shaped object at 22,000 feet over Kent. You may recall the reference on page 147 to other worldwide reports of these dark cylindrical objects seen from aircraft in mid flight.

The Kent missile was tracked briefly by radar at Heathrow airport but whilst attempts were made (and abandoned) to prove it was a rogue missile launch from a military unit the story was hushed up. Indeed, news of the sighting only emerged when the crew talked about it back in Italy some weeks later and the Ministry of Defence in London had to candidly admit that it was labelled 'a UFO'. The Civil Aviation Authority have since confirmed that this diagnosis still applies. April 1992 was to bring a much more voluble reaction to a second incident, seemingly unconnected with the above, culled from brief details in the 'air miss' report of the CAA (Civil Aviation Authority) that had then just been released. The tabloid press picked up on the story quickly. The *Sun*, for example (27 April) reported that 'UFO buzzes pilots' and said that a 'black lozenge like object' had 'missed a wing of a passenger jet by only 30 feet as it flew past at 400 mph.' Others were even more graphic. The *Daily Record* (28 April) claimed that 'A mysterious black UFO nearly brought down a crowded holiday jet' and the *Daily Mirror* (same date) stated that the UFO 'almost sent a holiday jetliner crashing to the ground.'

My views on this story were widely circulated, around the world as it turned out, but sometimes a crucial bit of what I said was missed out. The *Liverpool Daily Post* (28 April) had one of the best pieces, citing me as saying that 'this was a classic close encounter with a UFO', but then, adding the bit others excluded, that 'alien life forms are an extreme hypothesis'. However, most did report my concluding words that 'people tend to dismiss reports of UFOs, but when they come as close as this one did to causing a major accident they have to be treated seriously.'

In fact the air miss report itself (which we eventually secured) notes the following. The incident occurred at 17.45 hours GMT on 15 July 1991 and involved a Britannia Airways Boeing 737 jet flying at 14,000 feet on a descent into London Gatwick on a flight from Crete. Heading north north west the two man crew saw for just 1.5 seconds the small object ahead and at the same height as the plane. It passed 'less than 100 yards away' and 'at the most 30 feet above the level of the wing'.

London Air Traffic Control were immediately notified by the pilot and they reported obtaining a 'small primary radar contact astern of the aircraft'. The pilot assessed the 'risk of collision as high.' The Control noted that the pilot thought the object might be a balloon, and was only some eighteen inches in diameter (a fact many media sources left out). Such a size makes an alien probe rather improbable.

The primary radar target was ten miles behind the aircraft, but that was some seconds after the near miss, of course. This target was heading south east (the exact opposite course to the aircraft, just as the UFO had been) and was moving at 100 knots. This object then 'appeared to change heading' and went straight towards a second incoming aircraft! That seems to imply it was under controlled flight. London radar gave avoiding instructions to this jet, including a course change, to skirt the radar target. They saw nothing and the radar blip flew off out to sea.

The investigation of the incident found that a weather balloon was released from Crawley some twenty-six minutes before the incident and was at 27,000 feet and heading east. It was radar logged as moving with the wind at some 42 mph (only one third the speed of the radar-tracked object) and from these descriptions clearly was not the UFO seen.

They assessed all sorts of other options. The idea of a bin liner carried skyward was discussed but a temperature inversion at 4000 feet made it unlikely any such thing could have surpassed that height. Whilst home-made black balloons had been tracked as reaching up to 7000 feet and were thought to be potentially capable of going higher (although this was debated by other sources), no regular launcher known to the CAA had released one. But the report did note that such sightings were becoming 'more prevalent in the south and south east of the country'.

The radar target was moving like a powered aircraft or helicopter not a balloon and as a result of all these factors the authorities noted that 'this air miss was best described as a confliction between the Boeing 737 and the unidentified object. Whilst members were unsure what damage could have occurred had the object struck the [aircraft] the general opinion was that there had been a possible risk of collision.'

It took some time to get access to this important data, by which point the media had long lost interest in the story. Indeed the highbrow press attempted (quite wrongly) to imply that the tabloids had distorted the truth. They had failed to mention the small size, but that is all.

The Times (28 April) referred to it as a 'silly season' story –

hardly a fair reflection on the concerns about this near collision. They accused the CAA of being 'incautious' – presumably thus supporting a cover-up of dangers facing air traffic. Both *The Times* and the *Daily Telegraph* chose not to mention my highly syndicated press comments about the matter and claim that a spokesman for BUFORA had accepted that the UFO was a balloon.

Consensus opinion within BUFORA's investigation team is that this must be seen as unlikely, given that the radar target flew faster than any windborne object and changed course, plus the improbability that a small balloon would have been tracked on radar anyhow. All the other factors from the investigation imply this was probably not the explanation.

Of course one cannot rule this idea out, certainly given the home-made balloon experiments reported before. However, even if this is what was seen then its close proximity to a holiday jet in a way that the CAA very clearly found to be hazardous does not excuse the trivialized laughter that the story received merely because some tabloids went overboard with their use of language. It was unidentified, it was flying and it was undeniably an object – so a UFO is precisely what it was.

However, of much greater concern is the way this case was seen in complete isolation. For when put alongside the almost identical Alitalia report from just three months before it shows a very worrying pattern. And, as we were to discover, these two cases did not stand alone.

We found others by pure chance. In attempting to obtain interviews with the crew of the 15 July 1991 incident BUFORA investigator Ken Phillips was given the wrong airline by me by mistake over the phone. This turned out to be rather fortuitous because that airline, Dan Air, had been involved in a third mid-air encounter during summer 1991!

On 6 August Derek Harper, the flight safety officer for Dan Air, told Phillips that there was an incident on 17 June 1991. We have learnt that four passengers and possibly some crew saw a dark projectile fly close by aircraft call sign 'Echo Lima' on a flight from London Gatwick to Hamburg. It was passing through 5000 feet over the Essex/Suffolk area at the time. The UFO came very close by the wing of the Boeing 737 jet. Again the sighting was immediately reported by the pilot to London Air Traffic Control, who this time had no radar tracking to confirm. An official report was made and Phillips has succeeded in tracing one of the witnesses. Harper, for Dan Air, told us that they had received no explanation for the incident.

Finally, whilst Phillips was making enquiries about these matters with the Joint Air Miss Section at RAF Uxbridge, Group Captain John Maitland noted that only the 15 July incident had been reported as a near miss (although the report written by the Alitalia captain infers this was too), but amazingly advised that there was a fourth incident! On this occasion, 1 June 1991, another aircraft (we believe a British Airways Boeing 737) had a visual encounter with a dark cylindrical object somewhere north of London. Enquiries into this matter are still proceeding.

It does seem utterly incredible that there were at least four mid-air incidents of such similarity in a period of just twelve weeks during summer 1991. All seem to have occurred in good weather and daylight and at least one, probably two, were what most would call near misses. Four different airlines were involved, all carrying unenlightened passengers. At least two of the close encounters were tracked on radar and termed UFOs by all relevant authorities.

This must pose serious questions. Firstly, why are the travelling public generally not being told about these potentially hazardous incidents? One emerged by accident and only because it involved a non-British crew. Another was found by chance by a media source buried away in an air miss catalogue. The other two were not publicized at all and as we saw before there were other similar cases in Australia and the USA.

This must make it necessary to ask whether, if we can discover four British cases in just three summer months of 1991, how many really took place during that period of time over southern England alone? Indeed, how many have happened since 1991 and how often is this sort of thing going on in the crowded skies all over the world?

Even if the UFOs do turn out to be balloons I think it is right that UFOlogists fight to expose this aerial menace.

Zoological Mysteries

There are monsters on this earth. At least, that is the opinion of many cryptozoologists, the name given to hunters after these strange and unidentified creatures. Whilst it might be assumed that no large, undiscovered animal could possibly exist without having been captured and put on display in a zoo, that is not a view fully supported by the facts. New species are being found on a regular basis and some of these are quite large. There are vast areas of relatively unexplored land and the world's oceans, which cover two-thirds of our inaptly named earth, are almost as unknown to us as is the surface of Mars.

It ought to be no real surprise that people still dream, like Arthur Conan Doyle's Professor Challenger, of finding a lost world peopled by dinosaurs. Indeed, there are those who believe they even know where this lost world is located. It is in the African Congo around the Lake Tele region, where since the first missionaries braved the poisonous snakes, carnivorous animals and, in places cannibalistic natives there have been stories about the *mkoele mbembe*. This is said to be a creature the size of a rhinoceros with a long neck that eats mainly the molombo plants from tall trees by the water, rather like a giraffe. In many respects the animal sounds like a remnant of the dinosaur era, that officially ended over sixty million years ago. Indeed some think it is a brontosaurus, although most specialists argue that if it exists it is an evolved version of a smaller creature, possibly an atlantasaurus.

There have been missions into the jungles, even scientists who claim to have seen it. In 1983 one filmed it for some minutes at only a few yards distance as it bathed in a pool. Or so he says. Sadly, this invaluable film was lost because the scientist forgot to switch from macro setting and only produced an out-of-focus mess!

But in 1992 a British expedition of ex-army explorers set out there on their second mission to find this lost world. The team was led by Bill Gibbons, whose first trip in 1986 had involved several near misses and various brushes with the authorities and natives, who tend to exhibit great fear when the thought of entering this region is mentioned.

The 1992 trek was really only a reconnaissance for what is planned to be 'Operation Congo 1994' and the idea was to test the feasibility of combining a dinosaur hunt with a humanitarian aid mission. Gibbons seems to think it is possible and hopes to get the funding to return and capture proof that the creature exists. But he will have to contend with the Congolese government who have decided quite properly that, as there is a fair chance they may have one of the world's zoological treasures on their hands, it must be protected. So visitors will have to agree only to film it, not to try to take it prisoner. Such a species protection order on a dinosaur sounds like something out of a Steven Spielberg movie, but is to be applauded none the less.

Of course, these are those who think you do not have to take the enormous risk of trekking into steamy jungles to find a dinosaur. They argue that one can be found amidst the much more hospitable surroundings of the Scottish highlands. But then, the Loch Ness monster itself had a torrid time during 1992. Indeed someone claimed that he was the monster!

Eighty-six-year-old Lambert Wilson was the source of the story. In August, after new sightings, he broke half a century of silence to advise the *Daily Mail* that he was the long-necked creature that appears in the world's most famous photograph, circulated everywhere in 1934 after it was taken by a surgeon (the unrelated Robert Wilson) by the loch-side. Lambert says that he bought a sea-snake head from a joke shop and obtained the help of a theatrical costume-maker to forge a realistic monster head. There had by that point been sightings off and on for four or five years but no good photographs. So he decided to swim under water, parading the head for the benefit of a knot of people on the shores. He says he had put peepholes in the monster's neck through which he saw photographs being taken. At one stage someone even threw stones at him. Then he submerged and swam out of sight leaving the world with pictures that were the start of decades of monster-watching.

In fact, coincidentally, just a few months before this revelation arch monster sceptic Steuart Campbell, who authored the critical but well respected book *The Loch Ness Monster: the evidence* (Aquarian Press, 1984), had already addressed the subject of how the legend started in a piece for the *Skeptic* (March 1992). Campbell, quite correctly if Lambert Wilson's story is true, had long argued that the surgeon's photograph was inconsistent with a large monster. He analysed the wave ripples from the neck and the angles from which cameras could point at the site and effectively established that the object in the picture was much smaller than suggested, perhaps only a foot or so long. This may be a slight underestimate, but his essential argument could well have been vindicated by Wilson's admission.

Campbell has also looked at some of the early sightings in the period 1933 to 1935 and seems to have found some suggestion that rumours were deliberately fanned based on less-than-genuine sightings. If true, then the entire basis of the modern belief in a creature within Loch Ness may have been undermined during 1992.

New evidence in the Loch

But 1992 had an upside for monster lovers. There was plenty of positive evidence from new investigations that something odd might really be within the peaty depths of these Scottish waters.

Each summer the Loch Ness project rounds up volunteers with their sleeping bags and packed lunches to scour the waters. There is plenty to do because very little is known about the more mundane zoological goings-on in this huge and deep stretch of water gouged from a rift in the earth's surface and sealed off since the ice age. New help is always being sought (see address on page 186).

The major research of the year was Project Urquhart, partly set up by long-term monster hunter and television newsreader Nicholas Witchell. This used sonar to search for echoes of large moving targets deep beneath the surface. It seems from all estimations that if there really is a large animal in the loch it lives in the thousand-foot depths and surfaces only rarely, thus explaining why no bones are ever found.

At 7.04 p.m. on 27 July 1992 the project appeared to pay off when a 'large and solid-sounding' target was picked up on the

Norwegian vessel carrying the equipment and as attested by Bon Manson of Simrad, the company whose equipment was being utilized. The team had stressed that they were not really monster hunting but surveying the fish and other life in the waters and, in particular, mapping the floor of the Loch, but did indeed record something strange between Foyers and Invermoriston. The sonar operator Thor Edland confirmed it was 'larger than anything else spotted in the loch and very strong' noting that the equipment locked on and tracked it for a couple of minutes some fifty feet under the water. Of course, nothing specific was seen and sadly no recordings have emerged as this equipment was not working at the time.

The team were understandably cautious about making too much out of this echo, pointing out that spurious effects do sometimes occur. But the general view seems to be that this object was too large and solid for that. They hope to secure more funding to make further surveys, particularly as they made real progress, proving that the loch is far deeper than the previously estimated 750 feet and that caves, long suspected to exist and perhaps even hide monsters, do not exist. However, they did find a real puzzle – a line of 'bumps' on the lake bed about 600 feet down and about 200 feet apart. They seem too regular not to be artificial in origin but nobody has worked out what they might be.

Two weeks later, the *Daily Mail* (12 August) revealed the somewhat fuzzy picture of a neck emerging from the water taken a few days earlier. A 45-year-old man secured the picture with a Boots 'instamatic' type camera whilst camping near Fort Augustus. He claimed it surfaced whilst he was washing in the water after breakfast and he watched as it swam some hundred feet away, at one point opening its mouth and creating the impression it might even eat him! The photographs were shown to a zoologist at the Natural History Museum, who remarked that it was silly season, to the RAF photo laboratories, whose flight lieutenant Caroline Smith concluded they had not been touched up, and the Kodak laboratories, who as they usually do said only that they were genuine pictures of something but declined to comment on exactly what.

Even then the fun was far from over, for camcorder film of the monster was to follow swiftly. A man from Glasgow, who again wanted anonymity, filmed an effect in the water near Urquhart

Castle, a favourite monster haunt. It is best to describe this film (taken mid August on an unknown date) as an effect, because it certainly does not show a monster in any traditional sense. Rather, a rippling lump and occasional white blob appear to amble around the surface in a 'cycling' motion, as one commentator has described it. Malcolm Robinson of SPI carried out an enquiry and was told that the original video had been accidentally destroyed by a television company who wanted to screen it. Very sad, if true. But copies do exist.

Mrs Betty Gallagher of the Loch Ness Monster Exhibition situated by the loch was impressed but reasonably suggested that she thought it just a wave. Professor Archie Roy from Glasgow University, an astronomer and hunter after mysteries like UFOs and crop circles, wisely preferred to keep options open but said he did not think it looked like a wave. Support for the wave concept came from those who know the waters well. Adrian Shine, long-term monster hunter, said he had seen something similar earlier in 1992 and that the poor contrast of the film adds to the illusion. He believed it was a boat wake. Steuart Campbell agreed. He told Robinson (as reported in *SPI Enigmas*, November 1992) that the video shows 'a rare interference effect between [boat] wakes ... when two waves meet they cause a large hump of water to appear ... this is the first time this wave effect has ever been caught on film so far as I know.'

However, Archie Roy's colleague at Glasgow University, Professor Peter Meadows, is perhaps well qualified to judge if it could be an animal as he is a senior lecturer in marine biology. He reported that he was initially rather sceptical but on close inspection of the video was unable to match it up with any type of animal that he had seen. But then one wonders if he has had the experience of seeing the apparently rather unusual effect created by interfering boat wakes that Campbell and Shine talk about and which has supposedly provoked several sightings of Nessie in the past.

Other water monsters

Loch Ness is not the only body of water that reputedly has a strange inhabitant. In fact they are very numerous. Most large lakes in northern latitudes have some legends associated with them.

The AFU group from Scandinavia report an incident on 29 April 1992 in Lake Storsjon in mid Sweden. A group of thirteen students from Ostersund were on Froson island watching building work on a new bridge when they saw something rise from the water 600 feet from the shore. Accounts describe it as about twenty-five to thirty feet long with both a head and tail as it drifted on the surface for about fifteen seconds and then submerged. One witness was angry afterwards because he had his camera with him but was too shocked to take what he later said would have been a picture of a lifetime. It seems that bridge construction workers saw the creature as well. Sketches show that it had a hump-like body, dark brown in colour, and a long serpentine neck, almost identical in fact to some of the better views people claim to have had of Nessie. Lake Storsjon was ice-bound apart from a small area surrounding the bridge and, although there have been various sightings of the creature before, these have always been in the summer months when the surface is exposed.

Photographic evidence was obtained on 4 January 1992 at Lake Ikeda in Kyushu, Japan. In fact it was a video film and a still was reproduced in *Fortean Times* (February 1992). The camcorder operator was Hideaki Tomiyasu who was driving on the shores in late afternoon with his family when they saw a 'log' in the water. Stopping to look more closely it appeared to be a slightly humped back of an animal perhaps twelve feet long. They watched it surface and resurface and filmed for some time, too long for this to have been a wave or wake. They spotted brown and yellow stripes and called out that it must be 'Issie', the local name for the monster. The family estimate that the animal must have been some thirty feet long under the surface but it never fully appeared. Finally, a speedboat arrived on the scene and, as if frightened, the object ducked beneath the waves for the final time.

Hairy man monsters

All over the world there are reports of another type of monster, as consistently seen as these lake monsters. It goes by a variety of local names and even seems to have different skin colours to blend in with the local surroundings, itself suggestive of a real animal.

In Australia it is often yellowy-brown and goes by the name of the Yowie. Mountain climbers in the Himalayas say it is white and hairy and the Tibetan name Yeti (from Yeh-Teh or rock creature) has stuck, as has its more affectionate appellation 'abominable snowman'. In the forests of western USA it is darker brown and has attracted the friendly term 'bigfoot'; although Native Americans have known it for centuries as Sasquatch. But clearly all these things refer to the same type of entity, a manlike and very hairy ape around eight feet tall, powerfully built and often described as having a smell like a bad public toilet. In 1992 a team of scientists from Russia and France set off on an expedition to hunt what seems to be the European version, seen in the Caucasus mountains and locally known as the Almasty.

Mark Opsasnick reported in *Strange Magazine* (Fall 1992) that bigfoot was pretty active in the USA during the year. Indeed sightings began on 1 January at Sandy, Oregon, when a figure was seen to cross a road and run up a snow bank into the woods. It was reddish brown and between seven and eight feet tall. A close-up sighting near Mount Saint Helens on 4 January added new details. The nine-foot tall figure was said to have enormous breasts and a bloated stomach and either to be in bad need of a diet or pregnant! Meanwhile long-time bigfoot hunter Paul Freeman, who claims to have seen it many times, was even luckier in the Blue Mountains of Washington because on 14 April he got fifteen seconds of it lumbering away on his Sony camcorder. Unfortunately it was well in the distance at the time and this example was smaller than most of the others, being only about six-and-a-half feet tall.

However, the incident of the year, on 12 June in the early hours of the morning, was far removed from these north west American forests. It involved a three-man expedition led by Julian Freeman-Attwood which was then in the bleak snow-covered glacier of a peak in Mongolia, mid way between Siberia and China and hundreds of miles from any habitation. The climbers seem to have had a close encounter with what is here called the Almas. When they set up camp nothing was anywhere near them. Upon decamping at 4 a.m., only a few hours later, an eerie sight greeted them: a trail of heavy imprints winding their way up the snowdrift towards the top of the glacier. Photographs taken at the time show that the creature that left the prints was heavy, estimates from the depth suggest over ninety kilos, and had three toes and a foot size much larger than a human's. There was no time for the snow to have melted and artificially increased the size of normal animal prints, such as a bear's, a commonly offered explanation when such tracks have been found by previous expeditions. The fact that the time of appearance of the tracks can be accurately noted and that this was during the night all argue that what was filmed upon awakening was an accurate record of the markings that the animal actually left.

Plans are afoot in 1993 to launch a major filming expedition all around the world to try to obtain firm evidence of this creature.

Big cats ... the British beast

There is nothing quite as dramatic as a bigfoot in the British Isles but a zoological mystery of similar proportions revolves around the phantom big cats that have been roaming the countryside for decades. They were active once again during 1992.

There is no place where these animals particularly concentrate. 'Cat flaps', as researcher Andy Roberts calls them, are prone to happen almost anywhere and to be of assorted descriptions, often said to be black panther-like pumas and sometimes lynx or even leopards. Most commonly these are not really big cats at all but large dogs. However, there has been some evidence of a strain of large feral (or wild) domestic cat that may even have interbred with native Scottish wild cats (not dissimilar to domestic cats) and produced a large wild cat not as big or ferocious as a puma but odd none the less. There have also been some incidents where big cats have been found to be escaped pets whose owners had no licence for dangerous creatures and so did not own up when they went on the run.

However, the evidence is mounting that some sort of large cat akin to a puma might really exist in small numbers, just as one of England's best-kept zoological secrets is the small colony of wallaby known to have survived in the Derbyshire Peak District near Buxton. The problem is that no corpse or bones of an indigenous British big cat is ever found, thus leading to the supernatural image that surrounds it and the term 'phantom' sometimes appended. Indeed, some have mused, perhaps they are ghostly remnants of the large animals that did once roam the country tens of thousands of years ago? However, phantoms are notoriously difficult to film and the big cats in Britain have achieved some notoriety on celluloid.

In January 1992 reports resurfaced of the 'Exmoor beast', said to be a family of puma-like creatures on the Devon moors. One man reported how he lost his Christmas dinner to a huge brown cat near Tiverton and there are several cages being set up to try to capture the culprit. So far there has been no success, although one sighting told of a big mother cat and several cubs being seen together.

The most impressive evidence came from around Kidder-minster in Worcestershire, where big cats had been seen since 1962. Bob Lawrence of a local wildlife park had identified prints as akin to those of puma and verified that the reported sightings match this diagnosis. However in May Nick Morris stalked the animals near Great Witley and was rewarded with the opportunity to take two photographs. Lawrence said that the animal filmed was too small to be a puma but suggested an African golden cat instead.

On 9 April, as British voters were re-electing John Major, a large cat was seen in a tree at West Hampstead, London. A cat expert from London Zoo was called in by the police. He was satisfied by the witnesses' stories and suggested the animal sounded like a jungle cat or puma. He pointed out that in African cities big cats often stay hidden for months, raiding dustbins at night and only being a threat to small pets, never humans.

It may be that these sightings of what are sometimes called ABCs (alien big cats – in the sense that they are 'alien' to the country in question) might lie behind outbreaks of mutilated sheep and cattle which do plague some areas.

The mutilators

Early in 1992 there were reports of sheep being found badly mutilated in the Orkneys. Although superficially you might assume that this would suggest more evidence of big cats on the loose, there is a tendency within the supernatural community to look deeper than that and read stranger things into such phenomena. Indeed, because in places (though not these Orkney reports) the mutilation appears to be precise, almost surgical, with organs removed and an absence of blood, the idea that some sort of alien genetic experiment might be under way has taken root and the phenomenon is often linked with alien abduction claims about body samples taken from humans. However, in many cases the explanation is simpler than that. Sometimes it is merely evil-minded people, as seems to be the case with some horse and pony slayings in the West Country. In countries such as Puerto Rico, where mutilations to chickens are common, the blame is often laid on ritualistic cults practising voodoo or even satanism.

Quite a debate about the Orkney mutilations developed in the pages of *Northern UFO News* during 1992 and local vet Dr Peter Talbot checked them out without establishing that anything untoward was happening. There had been some reports of mutilations caused by killer mink which were gaining a foothold in Britain and wreaking havoc in a few places, but not in the Orkneys. Perhaps a few isolated cases had simply been exaggerated into a radical wave of happenings.

Expert in the field of the 'animal mutilations' mystery is Linda Moulton Howe, an American television producer, whose CBS documentary *A Strange Harvest* won international acclaim and who now believes that the phenomenon is associated with some very strange areas. She has been over to look at English crop circles and there have been a couple of isolated cases of mutilated animals, in particular a horse, found near a circle site. However, I tend to think that this is more likely to be connected with some of the fringe people who have clung to the coat tails of the publicity that the circles attract and who might have thought that this sickness would gain attention.

Linda Moulton Howe points out that she never set out to find 'alien' links with the American multilations, but that the pattern simply forced itself upon her. She presented some gruesome physical evidence of cattle with organs removed in clean, bloodless cuts at a lecture to the Fortean conference in Nebraska in May 1992. Then she reviewed the American cases for the year in *MUFON Journal* (October 1992).

There was a wave of these events in Oklahoma and

surrounding states in January and the usual claims of 'satanic ritual' were proposed, but never established, as is customarily the case. Chuck Pine took tissue samples from one mutilated steer in Caldwell, Kansas on 1 February and these were studied by Moulton Howe and pathologist Dr John Altshuler. Haemoglobin was apparently cooked and other cellular changes found in both this case and other examples from elsewhere. This may suggest that whoever is doing the surgery is using precision instruments based on high temperatures.

Mutilations continued throughout the year, often in terrible detail, such as a cow's rectum or vagina scooped out. In many of the locations there were reports of strange pulsing lights in the sky above the fields where animal remains were later found.

There have been some reports of aliens in contact with cattle. The most graphic is a case from the banks of the River Weaver near Frodsham (the rather appropriately named Devil's Garden) when four men saw entities emerge from a landed object with a cage and place this around an immobilised cow, moving bars up and down as if taking measurements before taking it away. The men fled in panic. Moulton Howe also had a case where a woman and her daughter say they were abducted by a UFO and aliens and observed cows being levitated into beams of light and sexual and other body organs removed. Under hypnosis one of the witnesses here reported that the experiments she saw carried out were very important for survival – both of the aliens and humanity!

1992: A Review of the Year

What the psychics said

It is always interesting to compare what actually happens with what those brave psychics who dare make specific predictions have said about a year before it starts.

Before 1992 there was growing concern about the Middle-Eastern conflict, quickly resolved as it happens. So the prophecies about that largely faltered. Intriguingly a new interpretation of the prophecies of Nostradamus pointed to the Balkans as the coming centre of crisis.

Nostradamus, a French doctor in the seventeenth century, wrote a series of cryptic verses which can be reassembled, translated and interpreted as you choose, a bit like seeing pictures in tea leaves. His various references to doom and gloom in 'year 1999 and seven months' when 'a great king of frightfulness will descend from the skies' has been variously interpreted as an atomic missile, a comet striking earth or aliens coming to fight a war of the worlds. Not even the date is certain ... does he mean July (the seventh month) or September (the seventh astrological month)?

Whatever the case the scholars were at work suggesting that the conflict in the former Yugoslavian states would escalate (which it did) and that atomic weapons would explode and cook fish in the seas around Greece and Turkey. That, thankfully, did not and seems very unlikely. If it happens few will thank the French doctor for this terrible forevision.

Mind you, we ought not to have too much faith in such prophecies. In Korea some 10,000 people did trust the Tami Missionary Church when it advised that the world would end on 28 October and the chosen 144,000 earthlings (themselves included) would be whisked into heaven whilst the rest of us faced doom and disaster. There were several suicides from followers who were unable to wait for the appointed day when all earthly goods would be useless. Sadly, one minister seems to have overlooked this financial problem when he took over three million US dollars in subscribed funds and purchased bonds that would not mature until 1995. This date was three years after the point when he had told parishioners the world and all banks would cease to exist.

Thousands of people were reportedly so convinced that the end was nigh that they sold all their goods and homes and were shattered when the 29 October dawned and all was well. However, oddly, this was the very day when Australians were told to watch the skies for Jesus. The Mission for the Coming Days announced his arrival and that it would coincide with a mass exodus to heaven. It didn't, but presumably this 24-hour discrepancy in the timing of judgement day had something to do with time zones and international date lines? Or does God not have to worry about them?

If predicting the end of the world is not a successful business, some psychics tried their hands at the rather more certain British elections on 9 April. The week beforehand all the polls were adamant that there was no way that the Conservatives could win again. John Major was out on his ear and Neil Kinnock on his way in to 10 Downing Street.

Psychics by the dozen all agreed. Ron Pollard, said to have been right about all bar one recent election, confidently announced there would be no overall victor but the Labour party would have most seats and take power. His principle source, according to *Psychic News*, 4 April, was a 'Chinese guide'. Astrologer Roger Elliot also did his thing, surveying the charts of fifty MPs and from this concluding a big swing to labour and a minority government for Mr Kinnock.

As history will for ever record, the ether proved a wee bit cloudy and not only did the massive swing not materialize but there was not even a minority parliament or hung verdict either. The Conservatives swept back to power defying all prophecies, from earthly and non-earthly sources.

However, there was some good news for the astrologers. Several of them were amazingly accurate about the 'Annus Horribilis' suffered by the British Royal Family and, in particular, by the heir apparent, Prince Charles, and his wife, Princess Diana.

In his book *Forecasting by Astrology*, published ten years before the fateful year, Martin Freeman assessed the future life of the then much in love Charles and Di with an insight that was astonishing. But, as I have discoverd, it was in fact mirrored by quite a few other astrologers who spotted the glaring signs a mile off. He says that '[1992] is another significant [year] for Prince Charles ... For an ordinary couple, turbulence in the marriage aggravated by broader life changes could be forecast ...' but adds that as we are dealing with such important figures the effects may well be more broadly felt. He adds that '1992 does not look a particularly easy year for the royal couple, [but] it is almost impossible for domestic or personal difficulty to be detached from the affairs of state.'

Well, you cannot argue that he got that one right. The domestic difficulties of the royals certainly did affect affairs of state, leading to books, media revelations, a television mini-series and the first serious questioning of the status of the monarchy itself amongst some parts of the community, culminating in the Queen herself noting that this year was the most horrible she had ever suffered. Seemingly, somehow or another, astrologers had spotted this bad time from Prince Charles's birth chart years before ... or was it just a case of one good prediction hardly making up for all the ones that got away?

Media merry-go-round

The media have a tendency to treat the supernatural with less than total seriousness. In the universal scheme of things it hardly matches up to weighty matters of state and sits somewhat uneasily between the love lives of television soap stars and recipes for health food. As a result it is sometimes difficult to know how seriously to take media stories about the paranormal. Even those which are based on fact are often treated less than scrupulously and I have myself suffered at the hands of the media more times than I care to recall. Often the results are amusing, wildly garbled versions of what I said. Occasionally it can cause considerable harm when a serious account is handled with as much journalistic pride as their comic strip.

That said I will look at some of the 'top' stories of 1992, fully stressing that there is often a very good reason why you have not already read about them in the detailed sections earlier in this book.

A rich store of such accounts is the tabloids of the *Weekly World News* (USA) and *Sunday Sport* (UK) category. In the past the latter has brought such gems as the first authentic photographs of heaven, the World War II bomber plane found dumped on the moon and (my favourite) the alien who turned a boy into a green lump looking like an olive, sadly eaten with a cocktail by the investigating police officer. Needless to say no paranormal researchers spent much time chasing around this world (or the next) after cases such as these.

A story that did the rounds in the US tabloids in spring 1992 was that Manchester United football club may have lost the league championship because of aliens. In fact, as the story went, they only drew a game against Chelsea 1–1 when a spaceship hovered over Old Trafford in February. This had sent crowds into a frenzy and upset the players. Luckily I can explain this. It is an exaggeration of a real situation, and I spent much of that night on the track of the phantom 'spaceship', as did a colleague of mine, actor Darryl Hedger, who was filming a scene for the hit television drama *Prime Suspect II* in the centre of Manchester that evening and called to tell me about the same 'alien craft' that he saw himself and immediately recognized for what it was.

In fact the UFO was an airship used for advertising purposes. It had been flying over the north west for days and been promoted (as a blimp) by generously proportioned comedian Bernard Manning. Consequently, few people did not know it was there, even though such airships were quite new to British skies and had provoked UFO sightings in previous weeks.

I was able to hear a local station's tape of the radio commentary made live from Old Trafford that night. The commentator, obviously not swept along by the tide of panic that wrecked his team's chances of success, described the scene in modest terms something like '... and the ball goes behind the line ... Ah, there's an airship flying over the ground ... Now it's a goalkick to ...'

Mass panic apparently has a different definition in newspaper dictionaries across the Atlantic.

However, there were some true stories with an unusual flavour. *Psychic News* on 28 March reported how a woman in

Dorset believed that her cat had psychic powers and, after advertising for a ghost writer (what else!) so as to tell the moggy's life story was approached by a man who tried to kidnap the prize pussy but was thwarted. I also loved their report about a very forward-looking prison in Worcestershire that was allowing an inmate to teach techniques of astral projection to some of the other long-term residents. It seems that in this way they were getting a taste of freedom by passing through the gates and walls without running the risk of extending their sentence if they attempted an escape in a more literal sense.

There was also an interesting case from Florida where a psychic sued a shopkeeper after she was hit on the head with a block of wood. As a result, it was alleged, she lost her ESP abilities. One of her major problems seemed likely to be how she could successfully demonstrate to a court that she had been previously able to see the future when she apparently was unable to predict, and thus avoid, her own accident...a real case of psychic powers cancelled due to unforeseen circumstances.

However, the best opportunity for a headline probably comes from a *Weekly World News* story. On 21 March they had a picture report of how the Loch Ness monster had been captured and then released when it was realized that the lovable prehistoric creature was about to give birth. The paper promptly ran a $1000 prize competition to name the baby! The winning entry turned out to be the ever-so-cute 'Dino-mite', thus allowing us to report that in 1992 'Nessie gave birth to Dinomite'.

On-screen supernatural

1992 was a good year for television and cinema treatment of the supernatural. It was certainly a controversial one, particularly in view of the event that created quite a serious rift – BBC Television's hotly disputed 'Ghost Watch'. You either loved it or hated it. 20,000 people called the BBC to give the latter verdict, but some asked for a repeat!

The programme was a spoof transmitted on Hallowe'en and billed as a drama in TV listings magazines, if not screened like one. It was handled so effectively, rather like Orson Welles's infamous 'War of the Worlds' radio play, that just as on that occasion, it created huge controversy.

The BBC made no bones about the fact that they were delighted it succeeded in scaring people more than they had hoped. Indeed, so popular did it prove that an American version is being planned. It used the well tried methods of drama-documentary at which British television excels. The fact that there had previously been totally serious 'Airport Watch' and 'Hospital Watch' programmes, where cameras reported live over a weekend on what was going on at airports and hospitals, must have added to the understandable confusion viewers had. This 'Ghost Watch' was very unwisely given too similar a name and format, causing viewers to question whether it was equally real. Even the telephone number from their highly popular 'Crime Watch' show was given out for a mock phone-in on air!

The production team argue that viewers should have spotted the TV magazine billings, or a small advance warning, but given these precedents it is not surprising that many did not – especially those who missed the first few seconds of the show. The fact that the programme used real factual programme presenters, including some best known for children's television work, must have also ensured that on a Saturday night quite a few children saw the one-and-a-half-hour fairy tale when on another night of the week it might have been too late for them.

The idea was to present the programme as a 'live outside broadcast' from a house invaded by a poltergeist. In fact, credited consultant was noted parapsychologist Guy Lyon Playfair, and the fictional case was clearly based upon his real investigations into a similar haunted house at Enfield. As in the BBC fiction, children there were the focal point. Playfair later told *Pyschic News* he could not understand why anybody took it seriously but added 'It should have been called "Carry on Poltergeist" and announced as a spoof then no one would have minded.'

But mind they did, in their thousands. Unfortunately, unless you were quite knowledgable about the subject, you would not spot clues linking it with real cases or other signs that the various participants were acting (sometimes well, sometimes not). Only towards the end did it degenerate into near farce (or terror, according to your predisposition).

Throughout it was generally so well done, with a professional parapsychologist, even a member of *CSICOP* (the American skeptics group beamed live by satellite) all realistically portrayed by actors, and jargon-filled discussions of what was going on, that it was easy to be taken in and believe you were watching a real investigation.

Most of the time it did not matter what you thought. You could just sit back and enjoy, especially when the children were caught cheating and various experts tried to justify their positions. Then, all hell quite literally broke loose, in a scary display of pyrotechnics as the evil dead took over the house, then possessed the television studio and host Michael Parkinson by leaping through cables as in the movie 'Poltergeist'.

There did not seem to be any explanation afterwards that it was all just a fiction. Viewers may well have thought a real disaster had taken place and, from the angry calls, clearly many did. It was this over-the-top ending that probably created more alarm than anything else.

However, when the dust began to settle it was revealed that a teenage boy had hanged himself after watching the programme. His family were in little doubt this was a factor. His suicide note mentioned ghosts. There do appear to have been other important circumstances and it would be unfair to prejudge any enquiry or imply that this tragedy should be laid on the shoulders of this television programme. Nevertheless this extreme reaction was symptomatic of the way there is a very fine line between sensible and incautious handling of the paranormal. Guy Playfair would, I hope, as a serious researcher, realize that he made a mistake in allowing his work and this subject to be hijacked in this way. Indeed he told *Psychic News* (14 November) that he felt the programme may have 'added considerable ignorance to the subject'. His co-researcher on the Enfield case was one of those who manned the phone line that the BBC asked viewers to call in on during the show. He told *Fortean Times* that at first people wanted to talk about their own experiences, but as the programme developed this became a stream of complaints and that this seemed to delight staff who felt that stirring people up was what they had wanted to do. He bemoaned the fact that they did not do a serious documentary on the Enfield case instead.

On a far less contentious note the USA 'main event' was a television mini-series called *Intruders*, screened over four hours and effectively a dramatization of Budd Hopkins' book of that title. This was a mildly fictionalized version of a case of alien abduction involving a woman in Indiana during the mid 1980s. Media reviews appear to have been very mixed and it is always difficult knowing whether it is right to gloss up a real case and add the spice that true life tends not to include. What makes a good paranormal investigation does not often make good television or cinema and to make the two come together sometimes involves an uneasy relationship. *Intruders* appears to have been one of the better attempts and it has already been aired in Australia, but to date is only available on video in Britain. It is possible a satellite TV screening will follow.

The problem such a dramatization introduces is that it familiarizes millions with the standard 'abduction' scenario as found in the USA and this is bound to influence future cases and, to a large extent, make subsequent abduction stories with similar features next to worthless as confirmatory evidence. On the other hand, you can say it adds to public awareness of the alien abduction mystery.

The BBC attempted to turn the paranormal into a fun television drama by making a series called *Moon and Son*, in which Millicent Martin played a psychic who helped police in France and England solve crimes as she did the rounds of the psychic fairs selling her tarot cards and crystal balls. The series proved entertaining and mildly diverting, but never fully absorbing from the viewpoint of its paranormal content. It also failed to win a big audience and a second series was cancelled. Mrs Moon's crystal ball apparently did not see that coming!

Books of the year

Every year produces many books about the paranormal, probably into the hundreds. It is impossible to mention them all, so this section is deliberately not intended to be a comprehensive review, merely a personal choice of some of the highlights.

Natural and Supernatural: A history of the paranormal
    Brian Inglis (Prism Books, Dorset)
    This is the last work by the late Brian Inglis, who was one of the most respected writers in the field. It is an excellent general introduction to the way in which the paranormal has been handled by science and society with many general lessons to be learnt.

The Circlemakers
Andrew Collins (ABC Books, Essex)
A travelogue through the author's personal investigation of crop circles with a focus on his new interpretation linked with orgone energy.

Crop Circles of 1991
Busty Taylor (Beckhampton Books, Wiltshire)
Private pilot Taylor provides a briefly annotated pictorial selection in glossy full colour of some of his best aerial shots from the most spectacular circles of the previous summer.

Shamanism and the Mystery Lines
Paul Devereux (Quantum Books, Berkshire)
Devereux introduces the concept of spirit paths around the world and the way tribal cultures and their shamans have a relationship with them.

Symbolic Landscapes: The dreamtime earth
Paul Devereux (Gothic Images, Somerset)
The companion volume that offers a radical reappraisal of the lines found criss-crossing the earth and linking ancient sites like Avebury.

The Stonehenge Solution
Dr Terence Meaden (Souvenir Press, London)
Meteorologist and physicist Meaden reinterprets the Stonehenge stone circle in line with his new idea that ancient peoples deified meteorological phenomena and built monuments in response to this.

Megalithic Adventures
Donald Cyr (Stonehenge Viewpoint, Santa Barbara, California)
A collection of the best articles from *Stonehenge Viewpoint* which reflects a wide range of thinking about stone circles, other earth mystery sites and earth energies.

Secret Life
Dr David Jacobs (Fourth Estate, London)
A detailed report on over sixty abductees who claim to have

been studied by aliens, usually examined through regression hypnosis. The details of their stories are analysed section by section.

The Omega Project
Dr Kenneth Ring (William Morrow, New York)
A radical new look at both near-death experiences (within which Dr Ring is a pioneer psychologist) and abduction victims (to which he is a relative newcomer). He assesses the parallels between them with an immense statistical analysis and offers a new theory to link them together.

Hidden Memories
Dr Robert Baker (Prometheus Books, Buffalo, New York)
An excellent sceptical look at the question of cryptomnesia, or how the mind can retain facts for years without realizing it, and how this process can combine with hypnosis and other altered states of consciousness to generate past-life claims, alien abductions, etc.

The Paranormal: Beyond sensory experience
Dr Percy Seymour (Arkana, London)
Seymour presents his 'world lines' concept, linking quantum physics with various aspects of parapsychology in an attempt to provide a unified theory of assorted events from precognition to ESP.

Nella: A Psychic Eye
Nella Jones (Ebury Press, London)
Nella Jones is a psychic detective who has used her ESP to assist with police enquiries. This tells the story of some of her more intriguing experiences in this field and other aspects of the paranormal.

In Touch with Eternity
Stephen O'Brien (Bantam Books, New York)
One of the world's best known modern-day Spiritualist mediums continues the story of his life and the messages that he believes he relays from the 'other side' with what he believes are new insights about the soul and the mind.

The Seventh Sword
Andrew Collins (Century, London)
Collins tells in great detail the saga of the quest to discover the six swords of Meonia and the assorted coloured stones, and the need and purpose behind the hunt for the final sword (which was already found!)

Closer to the Light
Dr Melvin Morse with Paul Perry (Bantam, New York)
Morse investigates the near-death experience amongst children, with a focus on those who have been his patients. The stories are sometimes heartbreaking but often inspiring and suggests pathways for new research.

In Search of the Dead
Jeffrey Iverson (HarperCollins, London)
This is a book of the BBC2 television series which looks at life after death from a number of viewpoints. The book combines both scepticism and belief-orientated approaches and is a good general overview of the field.

The UFO Encyclopedia
Jerome Clark (Omnigraphics, Detroit, Michigan)
Volumes 1 and 2 (with 3 due in 1993) constitute a major, unprecedented work which covers the UFO field in historical chunks (1 – 1980 onward; 2 – up to 1960 and 3 will plug the gap). Everything you need to know is in here in a series of papers that will be hard to equal.

UFO Crash at Roswell
Kevin Randle and Don Schmitt (Avon Books, New York)
The definitive (so far) report on the alleged UFO crash in the New Mexico desert in 1947 with the authors' first-hand attempts to track down (very old) witnesses and others involved. Makes a strong case that something happened. Whether you believe it was a spaceship is up to you.

Revelations
Dr Jacques Vallee (Ballantine Books, New York)
Dr Vallee presents the final book in a recent trilogy about UFOs, in which he offers a surprising series of ideas about how

disinformation at an official level might be obscuring a deeper level of UFO mystery where what we see on the surface (aliens and spaceships) may be an illusion masking something else entirely.

For the sake of completeness I add (without comment) details of my own 1992 publications:

From Out of the Blue: The UFO landings in Rendlesham Forest, Suffolk (Global Communications, New Jersey; also Berkley paperback)

Looking for the Aliens (with Peter Hough) (Cassell, London)

Spontaneous Human Combustion (with Peter Hough) (Robert Hale, London; also Bantam, UK, paperback and Berkley, US, paperback)

UFOs and How to See Them (Anaya, London and Sterling, New York)

The Top Ten Cases

Inevitably this is a personal selection but here are ten of the reports during 1992 which (at first sight) have impressed me. I summarize seven. The others (the Kent ghost, p.93, the Yeti footprints, p.161, and the Loch Ness sonar, p.164, are all discussed earlier. The cases are in no special order. Whether they all stay impressive remains to be seen!

1: Video film of strange light – Warrington, Cheshire

This puzzling affair began when a security camera at a shopping centre recorded a white blob of light in the early hours. The guard followed it with the lens as it moved up walls, through a yard and beside rubbish bins. Various ideas were assessed, such as luminous insects, an optical fault on the camera, car headlights from a motorway, but eight weeks later another camera at the centre pointing in an entirely different direction filmed the same thing. It was followed for over ten minutes until it vanished. The zoom lens gave us a massive soap bubble image filling one third of the screen at one point. Experiments showed it was in some way dependent upon the infra-red beams used in the camera system but scientists from three universities could offer no definitive solution. This was not a UFO, ghost or any typical paranormal phenomenon and whilst some tentative ideas were proposed during study in 1992 it remains unsolved.

2: Time distortion effect – Blackburn, Lancashire

This case involves what you might think a forward time slip but termed by psychologists a 'false awakening'. A woman woke up, got out of bed and noted the time was 11.22 a.m. on her digital alarm. She went to the bathroom, glancing over the banister to see if a letter she was expecting had arrived in the mail. There was no post at all. She used the bathroom, had a glass of water but noted that all ambient sounds (apart from the toilet chain and sink) had vanished. Returning to the bedroom she decided to 'grab' another half hour's sleep. The next thing she knew she was being woken by her husband with the letter. Had it come in the second post, she asked? In fact, he pointed out, it was then just 9.10 a.m.

3: Alien abduction – Melbourne, Australia

A six-year-old boy described how little entities with grey skins and large black eyes had come into his bedroom and 'shone a torch' at him. He was then paralysed but was told 'in his mind' that he should not be afraid. They examined him and placed a probe up his nose. His mother also recalled a force trying to pull her out of bed and dreams that these were 'pixies'. Under regression hypnosis she recalled a childhood abduction in 1961 where she had been taken to a room and examined with a probe pushed up her nose. Late in 1991 they had returned but she had refused to go. They used a 'silver knife' to scrape the skins of both herself and her husband and said this was the last time 'for a while'.

4: Alien abduction – Hungary

This phenomenon is crossing cultural boundaries. In September 1992 I discovered several cases of great similarity in this former Communist state. In one, on 24 January 1992, a 50-year-old woman from Mezobereny saw a small dark oval entity cross her room and then vanish. A few hours later she was taken from her bedroom by an orange beam of light into a room where she found herself naked, as were about a dozen others, children and young women. After losing all memory of what happened next she found herself back in her bed, several hours having passed. But three round red blotches appeared on her abdomen and remained for some days. She also felt extremely tired and unwell. The physical effects were photographed.

5: UFO sighting – Brignoles, France

At 3.25 p.m. on 8 July 1992 a French helicopter on a routine army flight from Le Luc to Aurillac encountered a strange object over the town of Brignoles. It was black, elongated, with triangular ends. The aircraft was at 6000 feet below a cloud of 10,000 feet. The crew estimated the object to be just below cloud, going south at 300 knots with the wind, size 15 feet. It was reported to radar at Aix-en-Provence, who tracked nothing. A civil flight passing over (above clouds) also saw nothing. This case is very similar to the various British mid-air encounters (see page 153).

6: Precognition – Strasbourg, France

Psychic Dave Mandell appears to have tragically foreseen his third air disaster in as many years. He claims to have seen a non-fatal accident involving a jumbo over Darwin, Australia, in 1989 and a crash in Thailand in 1991. On this latest occasion, Mandell saw 'an airliner struggling to gain height'. A second appeared behind 'flying low' but the one in front was 'flying purposely slow in order to force the plane behind to slow up'. It was desperately 'trying to regain a safe height' but was prevented by the phantom twin jet in front. Disaster following when they collided. A few hours later he was photographed holding a painting of his dream in front of the Sudbury's Hill Barclay's bank with a display that shows the date and time, proving (*Psychic News* felt) it was some three hours before an aircraft crashed that night. The livery of the jet closely resembles that in the picture and it was forced to fly too low, commentators speculated, by a possible error in a 'fly by wire' system. Because of this it was unable to avoid hitting Monte Sainte-Odile. Mandell thinks the first aircraft in his dream leading the second to disaster was a symbol for the faulty autopilot. When the accident report appears we may know if he was even more correct.

7: Psychic Detection – California, USA

Sadly I met Scott Rogo just once. Like most researchers I considered him the epitome of what our work is all about. His many books stand as a great testament to his life's work, tragically cut short by murder at his San Fernando Valley home in August 1990. Tim Moss, the detective who wrestled with the case, told *Fate* magazine after the January 1992 trial how he had received 'help' from psychics, some claiming to 'sense' Rogo trying to assist the enquiry. Armand Morcotte was particularly accurate. A major unpublicized clue was a blurred fingerprint on a drinks glass found at the scene. Forensic felt it was worthless, but Moss pressed for its study. The print was found to be readable and linked with the main suspect, who was then found guilty of second degree murder at the trial. Before this Morcotte had written to Moss stating that the murderer's print was on a drinking glass … 'Kind of eerie' is Moss's diagnosis.

References

The following addresses cover some of the groups and magazines referred to in the text. Hopefully, you will find these useful for further investigation. They should add to your knowledge of the paranormal.

If, however, you would like to report anything strange you can do so (in confidence if you request) via: 37 Heathbank Road   Stockport SK3 OUP

AFU
  Box 11027 600   11 Norrkoping   11 Sweden

Association for Past Life Research and Therapies
  PO Box 20151   Riverside   CA 92516   USA

ASSAP (Association for the Scientific Study of Anomalous Phenomena)
  20 Paul Street   Frome   Somerset   BA11 1DX

Awareness
  11 Ousley Close   New Marston   Oxford   OX3 0JS

British and Irish Sceptics (The *Skeptic*)
  PO Box 475   Manchester   M60 2TH

BUFORA (British UFO Research Association) (*UFO Times*)
  Suite 1   2C Leyton Rd   Harpenden   Herts   AL5 2TL

Bulletin of Anomalous Experience
  2 St Clair Avenue West   Suite 607   Toronto   Canada   M4V 1L5

CCCS (Centre for Crop Circle Studies/*The Circular*)
  PO Box 146   Guildford   Surrey GU2 5JY

The Cerealogist
  c/o 20 Paul Street   Frome   Somerset BA11 1DX

CERES/TORRO (*Crop Circles/Journal of Meteorology*)
  54 Frome Rd   Bradford on Avon   Wiltshire   BA15 1LD

The Crop Watcher
  3 Selborne Ct   Tavistock Close   Romsey   Hants   SO51 7TY

CSETI (*ET Intelligence*)
  PO Box 15401   Asheville   NC 28813   USA

CUFOS (J Allen Hynek Center for UFO Studies/*International UFO Reporter*)
  2457 West Peterson Ave Chicago IL 60659   USA

Earthquest (ABC Books)
    Box 189   Leigh on Sea   Essex   SS9 1NF

Enigmas (SPI)
    41 The Braes   Tullibody   Clackmannanshire   FK10 2TT

Fate magazine
    PO Box 1940   170 Future Way   Marion OH 43305-1940   USA

Fortean Research USA
    PO Box 94628   Lincoln   NE 68509   USA

Fortean Times
    Box 2409   London   NW5 4NP

Gloucestershire Earth Mysteries
    PO Box 258   Cheltenham   GL53 OHR

Independent UFO Network (*UFO Brigantia*)
    84 Elland Rd   Brighouse   West Yorkshire   HD6 2QR

Lancashire Aerial Phenomena Investigation Society
    58 Torsway Avenue   Layton   Blackpool   Lancashire   FY3 8JZ

Linda Moulton Howe
    PO Box 538   Huntingdon Valley   PA 19006   USA

Loch Ness Project
    Loch Ness Centre Drumnadrochit Inverness Scotland IV3 6TU

Mars Mission (*Martian Horizons*)
    31-10 Skytop Gardens   Parlin   NJ 08859   USA

Mutual UFO Network (*MUFON Journal*)
    Box 12434   San Antonio   TX 78212   USA

MUFORA (Manchester UFO Research Association)
    6 Silsden Avenue   Lowton   Warrington   WA3 1EN

Northern UFO Network (*Northern UFO News*)
    37 Heathbank Rd   Stockport   Cheshire   SK3 OUP

Operation Right to Know
    554 Randolph St   Apt 2   Napa   CA 94559   USA

Orbiter
    43 Harrison Street   Reading   MA 01867   USA

PASU
    6 Oakhill Avenue   Greensburg   PA 15601   USA

Phenomena (*OVNI Presence*)
    SOS OVNI   BP 324   Aix-en-Provence   Cedex 1   France

PSI Researcher
    20 Paul St   Frome   Somerset   BA11 1DX

Psychic News
  2 Tavistock Chambers   Bloomsbury Way   London   WC1A 2SE
Slide (Street Light Interference)
  59 Tranquil Vale   London   SE3 OBS
Society for Psychical Research
  49 Marloes Rd   London   W8 6LA
Stonehenge Viewpoint
  800 Palmero Drive   Santa Barbara   CA 93105   USA
Strange Magazine
  Box 2246   Rockville   MD 20852   USA
Swamp Gas Review
  Box 1918   Winnipeg   Manitoba   Canada   R3C 3R2
The Ley Hunter (Earth mystery research)
  PO Box 92   Penzance   Cornwall   TR19 2XL
UFO Research Australia
  PO Box 2435   Cairns   QLD 4870   Australia
The Wild Places
  2 Victoria Rd   Mt Charles   St Austell   Cornwall   PL25 4QD

Library Archive facilities:

The Northern UFO Network files in Central Manchester are accessible for research by appointment; contact the MUFORA address.

The Center for UFO Studies have major reference materials in Chicago; contact the CUFOS address.

UFORA in Australia have a computer data base network via their address.

There is a major UFO book, magazine and archive library of UFO material at Newcastle Upon Tyne central library in England.

The Society for Psychical Research also have an extensive reference library which may be available to researchers on other paranormal topics.

In Britain only those interested in UFO and crop circle data can use a weekly news and information service, with reports that update current events. Operated by BUFORA at the standard rates for these information lines (which as of June 1993, is 36p per minute off peak – messages last about 3–5 minutes per week).

UFO CALL is on 0898 – 12 18 86

Index